The Successful Teacher's Survival Kit

The Successful Teacher's Survival Kit

83 Simple Things That Successful Teachers Do to Thrive in the Classroom

Dale Ripley

ROWMAN & LITTLEFIELD
Lanham • Boulder • New York • London

Published by Rowman & Littlefield
An imprint of The Rowman & Littlefield Publishing Group, Inc.
4501 Forbes Boulevard, Suite 200, Lanham, Maryland 20706
www.rowman.com

6 Tinworth Street, London SE11 5AL, United Kingdom

British Library Cataloguing-in-Publication Information Available

Library of Congress Cataloging-in-Publication Data
Names: Ripley, Dale, 1948– author.
Title: The successful teacher's survival kit : 83 simple things that successful
    teachers do to thrive in the classroom / Dale Ripley.
Description: Lanham, Maryland : Rowman & Littlefield, [2019] | Includes
    bibliographical references.
Identifiers: LCCN 2018043677 (print) | LCCN 2018045652 (ebook) |
    ISBN 9781475847079 (Electronic) | ISBN 9781475847055 (cloth : alk. paper) |
    ISBN 9781475847062 (pbk. : alk. paper)
Subjects: LCSH: Teacher effectiveness. | First year teachers. | Teacher orientation.
Classification: LCC LB1025.3 (ebook) | LCC LB1025.3 .R544 2019 (print) |
    DDC 371.102—dc23
LC record available at https://lccn.loc.gov/2018043677

Printed in the United States of America

This book is dedicated to the thousands of students
I have taught throughout my career.

By far you were my best teachers.

FOR PRESERVICE TEACHERS: Here's what lies ahead and how to successfully deal with the many surprises that you will encounter when you actually begin teaching.

FOR BEGINNING TEACHERS: Here are some easy-to-implement strategies that will help ensure you get off to a successful start in your teaching career.

FOR EXPERIENCED TEACHERS: Easy-to-implement ideas that will help you to smooth out the challenging areas in your teaching.

FOR SCHOOL ADMINISTRATORS: Quick, easy, and effective PD to improve teaching and learning in your school.

Contents

SECTION FIVE: WHAT YOU NEED TO DO DURING THE SECOND AND THIRD YEARS OF TEACHING, AND GOING FORWARD FROM THERE

Preface: Fish Discover Water Last

> It ain't what you know that gets you into trouble. It's what you know that just ain't so.
>
> —Mark Twain

Two young fish were swimming along one day, and they happened to meet a much older fish swimming toward them.

As he passed them, the old fish nodded and said, "Good morning boys, how's the water?"

The two young fish looked bewildered and simply swam on for a bit.

One of them finally looked at the other and asked, "What the heck is water?"

The trouble with teaching is that most people (parents, plumbers, pipefitters, lawyers, doctors, engineers, and so on . . . you get the point) believe they know a great deal about teaching. This is particularly true for preservice and beginning teachers. After all, by the time most people obtain their teaching degree, they have spent approximately sixteen years in classrooms.

The difficulty with this view is that it is fundamentally wrong. It assumes that because you were a *student* for sixteen years or so, you therefore have a good understanding of what it means to be a *teacher*. Dan Lortie (1975) called this "the apprenticeship of observation"—the belief held by many students (and a lot of adults) that because they have observed teaching for so many years, they know a great deal about teaching.

In my experience with preservice teachers and beginning teachers, I find that while most of them have been and are excellent *students,* none of them has any real understanding of what it means to teach and be a teacher. How could they? They have never taught—they have just observed teaching. This is analogous to me watching professional basketball on TV for several years and then thinking I can now qualify to play in the NBA. Not going to happen!

Like the young fish in our story, these novice teachers have been swimming in "school" for many years, but there is a great deal going on in successful classrooms that they simply do not see. That's the problem with watching great teachers—they make things looks so easy and effortless. But they're not!

It is my hope that through this book, I can help you "see" teaching in a more realistic and focused way; in a sense, that I can help you "discover the water" that is teaching.

Happy swimming!

Acknowledgments

While I wrote this book to teach teachers, it is my students who have taught me the most about teaching, and I would like to begin by acknowledging the thousands of students whom I have taught over the years. I thank you for all you taught me about what it means to be a successful teacher. I am so grateful for the experiences we shared.

I would like to thank my friend and partner Rae Gajadhar for her very thorough initial edit of this book.

I would also like to thank the preservice teachers who explored this book from the perspective of those looking to enter the teaching profession: Nicole Dundys, Angelene Huffman, Amy Moore, Caitlin Talty, and Margit Warner.

I would like to acknowledge the master teachers with whom I have had the pleasure to work and who so freely shared their stories and their edits with me. Their experiences and insights into our chosen profession have made this work so much stronger. Thanks to Garrick Burron, Bob Gagnon, Heather Jamieson, Ron Schlender, and Robyn Shewchuk.

And, finally, I would like to thank Dan Ripley for sharing his creative and artistic talents by providing the illustrations for this book. It can be difficult to come up with ideas as to how best to illustrate abstract concepts, let alone to then have the talent to draw them. Dan was able to do both, and for this I am most grateful.

Introduction: Establishing Legitimacy

In order to be a successful teacher, it is of critical importance for you as a teacher to establish *legitimacy* with your students as quickly as possible. In #23 of this text, I explore how critical it is for you to convince your students very early in the school year that what you have to teach them is of direct value and relevance to their lives. If you don't accomplish this, your students will be asking themselves, "Why should we listen to you? Why should we do what you want us to do?" They may not ask these kinds of questions aloud, but they will most certainly be thinking them—in particular as you move up the grades and the kids are older. These are not unreasonable questions.

In trying to model my own beliefs about the importance of establishing legitimacy, what I am attempting to do in this brief introduction is to establish my own "legitimacy"—to demonstrate to you that I have extensive experience in teaching, and that in sharing with you what I have learned through these experiences, there are some ideas here that will be of great value to you as you pursue your career as a teacher.

I have taught for almost forty years. I still love to teach, and I am still teaching today. I have taught children and young adults in elementary, junior high, and senior high schools. I have taught adults at community colleges and at technical institutes. I have served as the principal of elementary and secondary schools; and I have served as the superintendent of a small rural school district and a large urban school district as well. I have taught students in the inner city, in the suburbs, and on a First Nations reserve. I have taught rich kids and poor kids, brilliant kids and kids who struggled in school. I have written curriculum for government departments, and I have authored two social studies text books as well as published articles in educational journals and magazines.

I tell you this so you can see for yourself that I have had long and varied experiences in the field of education. I have found that I enjoy teaching all levels—from elementary students to adults—and I continue to derive a great deal of satisfaction from helping my students learn and reach their educational goals.

While I know that teaching bright, motivated kids is easy, I long ago discovered that it is not too challenging. I prefer teaching kids who other teachers may describe as "challenging." I have found that they bring out the best in me, that they keep me on my "teaching toes," and that if I am going to be successful with these kinds of kids, I need to bring my "A game" to class every day.

For the past number of years, I have been teaching preservice teachers at the University of Alberta. One of the many things these students have taught me is that they are starving for information about "what is it *really* like teaching in schools?" And even more importantly to them, "What do I need to know so I can be successful as a beginning teacher?" Survival is a major theme.

I found this desire among my students for "real-life" information in all of my preservice teacher education courses, and it came from virtually all of my students.

In response to this desire among my students for very practical, real-life information about what they needed to do to be successful as beginning teachers, I started to develop a collection of "teaching tips"—practical, real-life strategies that I had learned from over three decades of teaching experience in schools.

I start each of my classes with what has come to be known as "Rip' Tips"—tips that give my students very practical strategies regarding what to watch out for and how to survive and thrive as beginning teachers.

Over the years, feedback from my students regarding my "Rip' Tips" has been extremely positive. They e-mail me to tell me about how effective and helpful these tips are; they stop me in the halls of the Faculty of Education Building to tell me that they used some of these tips during their practicum or in their beginning years of teaching and that they worked really well. They tell me that they share these "Rip' Tips" with experienced teachers, who also find them to be invaluable.

Given that it took me almost forty years to learn these "Rip' Tips" and given that my preservice students have found them to be so useful, I have decided to share them with a larger audience of educators, both new and experienced.

I hope you find *The Successful Teacher's Survival Kit* and all of the eighty-three suggestions it offers to be as helpful to you as they have been to me throughout my career and to my education students.

Wishing you success in your teaching,

Dale Ripley, PhD

How to Get the Most from This Book

1. *For preservice teachers:* I suggest that you look through the table of contents and choose a dozen or so topics that interest you. You will probably want to start with the first section on what you need to know and do *before* school even begins. Try and visualize how you will work to implement these strategies into your teaching once you have a teaching contract and are getting ready for your own class. Then, as you become familiar with the first set of strategies that help you understand what you have to do to get ready before the school year starts, take a look at what you need to do on the first day, during the first week, and during the first month.

2. *For beginning teachers:* If you have just received your first teaching appointment and the school year has not yet begun, focus on the first section, and find out what you need to do to get ready for a successful year *before* the school year starts. If you have already begun teaching and are already into your first or second year, you will now have some sense of what seems to be working well for you in your teaching and what is not. Take a look at sections 2 and 3 of this book, and choose one or two strategies—the strategies that, if they were to be implemented successfully, would make the biggest positive difference in your classroom. These are the "pressure points" that you see and feel in your teaching—those areas of your teaching practice that, if improved, would result in the greatest return for you and your students.

    Now, work on these strategies for a while. When you feel you have implemented them effectively, choose the next couple to work on, and do the same thing. Over the course of a year, you will be able to implement many different strategies using this approach, and you will most certainly see positive results in your classroom.

And remember, if things are not going well in your classroom, the one thing that you have the most control over is *you* and what *you* do in your classroom. If you find that you are struggling, take a very detailed second look at the tips and strategies described in this book. Are you implementing them the way they are described here? If things are not going well on a regular basis, take a hard second look at *if* you are implementing these strategies and *how* you are implementing these strategies, and adjust accordingly. I am confident that you will see a great deal of improvement.

An important request from me to you: Please do *not* read this book from cover to cover and think that you will then understand and be able to implement the many suggestions contained herein. There are suggestions in this book that may not work for your particular group of students. There are strategies included here that will probably not make much sense to you when you first read them. However, these same ideas may become very clear after you have taught for a while and have had a few experiences like the ones described in a particular strategy. Give yourself both time and experience with teaching to fully understand the ideas that are being suggested here. Be patient with yourself please.

3. *For experienced teachers:* At this point in your career, you will have taught for a number of years, and you likely have the basics already in place. In fact, you may already be a very good teacher. Having said that, all good teachers know one great truth about teaching—we never get it absolutely right. I estimate that I have taught close to 40,000 lessons throughout my career—and none of them was perfect. We know that we can always learn more, that we can always improve in certain areas of our teaching craft.

For you, I would suggest that you read through and enjoy this book. There will be a great deal in here that you already know and can relate to—strategies that you already have in place. Having said that, I also suspect that there will be some aspects of your practice that have slipped a bit, facets that could use a little tune up. Or, there may be strategies and suggestions here that you simply never came across in your career that may prove useful. I hope this book helps you discover what these may be and how you can utilize them to make your classroom even better.

4. *For principals:* Good principals are always looking for ways to help teachers become more effective in their classrooms. This book has many excellent, easy-to-implement strategies that can have a very positive impact on student learning in your school.

Having been a principal for many years, I developed the practice of starting each staff meeting with a ten-minute professional development activity, where a staff member or I would introduce one teaching strategy that we would explore and discuss for the first ten minutes.

The strategies discussed in this book make a great start to a staff meeting. As a principal, simply choose one strategy (the one you feel your staff would benefit most from exploring) and then use it to start your staff meeting. Simply have someone read it, and then have your staff discuss the merits or challenges in the strategy as it would look in their classrooms. Decide how this might look like if you choose to implement it in your school. Quick, easy, and effective PD.

Section One

What You Need to Know and Do before School Even Starts

INTRODUCTION: THE IMPORTANCE OF THE TEACHER AND THE POWER OF POSITIVE THINKING

Congratulations! It actually happened—you have been offered your first teaching position. This is a very exciting time in the life of a teacher because now you finally get to have your very own class of students. If you are like most new teachers, you are excited, nervous, and a bit afraid. Or, perhaps, you have been teaching for some time and are looking to refine your teaching practice.

You need to be aware of how significant a role you play in the lives of the students in your classroom. Research shows us over and over again that effective teachers are the single most important factor that contributes to student success and achievement in schools. Although influences such as parent/caregiver support, class configuration and size, administrative support, and funding all impact how well your student will do, *the single most significant factor that impacts your students' success will be* you!

Spend a few moments thinking about these words by Dr. Haim Ginott (1972) from *Teacher and Child*:

> I have come to a frightening conclusion. I am the decisive element in the classroom. It is my personal approach that creates the climate. It is my daily mood that makes the weather. As a teacher I possess tremendous power to make a child's life miserable or joyous. I can be a tool of torture or an instrument of inspiration. I can humiliate or humor, hurt or heal. In all situations it is my response that decides whether a crisis will be escalated or de-escalated, and a child humanized or dehumanized.

(pp. 15–16)

There is a great deal of truth in those words. You—as the teacher—are the single most impactful element in your classroom. After spending over three decades teaching in schools, I can say with absolute confidence that over 90 percent of the great things that happen in any classroom happen either directly or indirectly because of the teacher. And I can say with equal confidence that over 90 percent of the discipline problems in any classroom *after September* happen because of the teacher.

In my many years of teaching, I have taught several hundred different classes. And they all had one thing in common. *I never had a bad class.* Some other teachers did, but not me. And *I never had a bad student* either. I only had good students, and "not yet good" students.

Why was that? Was I just lucky?

In 1956, Norman Vincent Peale published a book titled *The Power of Positive Thinking.* It was a runaway best seller, having been translated into fifteen languages with over seven million copies sold. In the book, Peale tells the story of meeting a man at a luncheon.

> I could not help admiring this dynamic man at the height of his power. "You amaze me," I commented. "A few years ago you were failing at everything. Now you have worked up an original idea into a fine business. You are a leader in your community. Please explain this remarkable change in you."
>
> "Really it was quite simple," he replied. "I merely learned the magic of believing. I discovered that if you expect the worst you will get the worst, and if you expect the best you will get the best."
>
> (p. 83)

I never had a bad class or bad students because I had stumbled upon what Peale's colleague called "the magic of believing." I believed that most kids wanted to be successful in school. I believed that most kids wanted their teacher to like, respect, and help them. I believed that most kids were flexible and that they would adjust to the expectations that I had for their behavior and their academic performance in my classroom. And guess what? They were!

In 2008, Dr. Terry Orlick, a sports psychologist from the University of Ottawa, published a book entitled *The Pursuit of Excellence,* which repeated Peale's message about the powerful impact our attitude can have in sports and in life as a whole. Orlick stressed the following reminders for those of us who want to excel at whatever it is we are attempting to achieve. These apply equally well to sports and to teaching.

- *Always positive thoughts*—because only positive thoughts will help you do the things you want to do in your classroom with your students
- *Always have positive images*—because only positive images of the things that you want do with your students will help you accomplish them
- *Always think "I can!"*—because only this kind of thinking will help you achieve what you seek in your teaching

- *Always opportunities*—because opportunities are present every day if you just take the time to notice
- *Always lessons*—because your students will teach you about teaching every day if you let them
- *Always step by step*—because you cannot become a master teacher quickly, you must learn your craft by taking small steps forward every day

You *can* have your "dream class" in your first year of teaching. In fact, *you can have your dream class every year you teach.* Perhaps they won't be so "dreamy" in September, but they certainly can be by Christmas if *you* do the right things and have the right attitude.

Sometimes, as a teacher, you can see potential in your students that the students themselves are blind to. In cases such as this, you see something that the students cannot see in themselves. If you are going to be successful as a teacher, you must have something that some students simply do not have. What is that? Faith in them. Faith in their potential. Faith in their promise—the "magic of believing" in their potential to achieve and their ability to grow.

If you were lucky enough to have great teachers for your university practice rounds of student teaching, you may have seen this in action. You will recall how easy they made teaching look. You will have arrived in their classroom several weeks or months into the school year, and their classroom routines were already well established. For the most part, the class just *flowed.* The teacher would ask the kids to do something, and the kids did it. The teacher would cue the kids to transition into a new activity, and the kids just transitioned.

It is a pleasure to observe these kinds of behaviors in the classrooms of master teachers, but it leaves new teachers with a colossal question: *how?* Just *how* did the teacher get their students to be so cooperative and the classroom running so smoothly? And that is one of the fundamental problems with student teaching—it does not start on the first day.

If you are a new teacher, you have likely never seen what a great teacher does *before school even starts* so that they and their classroom are ready. You have never seen what *the first day* and *the first week* of school look like in their classrooms—you do not get to see and understand all of the things that great teachers do to set the stage for a successful year for themselves and their students.

Well, that is what section 1 is going to show you—the things that effective teachers do *before school even begins* to maximize their opportunities for a successful year. Section 2 will take you through the first day and the first week. Section 3 will give you strategies to implement during the first month of the school year, and section 4 takes you through the remainder of the year.

Now, let's get started.

1. THE QUESTION YOU *MUST* ANSWER FIRST!

"Put first things first!" This seems so very self-explanatory, but very few teachers really put first things first, especially beginning teachers. So, what's the secret to actually doing this?

Step 1: You need to honestly answer this question: *What kind of a teacher do you want to be?*

1. A "paycheck teacher"—meaning a teacher who does the minimum amount of work necessary to collect their pay; or do you want to be. . .
2. A "good teacher"—meaning a teacher who genuinely likes kids, who works at preparing good lessons, who is aware of his or her students' personalities and needs, who gives good assessments to their students and gives reasonably prompt feedback to those students, and so on; or do you want to be. . .
3. A "great teacher"—meaning a teacher who loves his or her students, works conscientiously at getting to know students as individuals, and tailors each lesson to the particular group of students and their particular needs; a teacher who always gives his or her students back their marked assessments the next class; one who loves the subject matter he or she is teaching and whose passion for knowledge is infectious in the classroom. I could go on, but you get the picture.

Step 2: Before you can "put first things first," you need to figure out what *your* "first things" actually are.

This means that you truly need to determine what kind of teacher you want to be; what you want your classroom to look like in terms of student engagement in learning (Will your students be sitting and listening? Will they be exploring and experimenting? Will your students have a say in how the classroom looks in terms of décor and how it functions in terms of behaviors and rules?); and so on.

It is only after you have a *vision* for the kind of classroom you want and the kind of teacher that you want to be that will you be able to decide how to go about actualizing this vision. Only then will you truly know what your priorities will be.

Step 3: Work-life balance.

In the film *Freedom Writers* (based on the true story of Erin Gruwell and her teaching experiences at a high school in California), Gruwell is portrayed as being a very hardworking new teacher who is extremely devoted to her students. In the film, her commitment to her work and the long hours she puts into her teaching eventually lead to the breakdown of her marriage and ultimately to divorce. That is the movie. However, if you search Erin Gruwell on

Wikipedia, the site informs you that she started teaching in 1994. It also tells you that she and her husband of four years divorced in 1994. That is real life.

Understand that you have a life outside of teaching, and this life will make demands on you as well. Besides teaching, you may value time with family and friends, you may be raising your own children, you may cherish time with your partner, and you may have out-of-school interests that feed your spirit.

And you need to rest, rejuvenate, and take care of your physical and mental health. How does one manage all of this? How does a teacher find work-life balance?

Peter Coleman and Linda LaRocque (1990) wrote a book entitled *Struggling to Be Good Enough*. That is not a bad description of the first few years of teaching because even being "good enough" is challenging and is a great deal of work for all teachers, especially new teachers.

Step 4: Once you have done Steps 1 to 3, you will have begun to understand the difference between *urgent* and *important*.

There are many things in the daily life of a teacher that are urgent, that want to place immediate demands on your time (announcement over the school's intercom: "Ms. Smith, you have a call on line one"). Train the secretary to take messages. Do not constantly give in to immediate (aka urgent) demands on your time (fire drills and lockdowns being exceptions to this, of course).

Manage your teaching life according to *your needs* and *your priorities* as much as you can. Spend the bulk of your time and energy doing what fits into your personal vision and mission as a teacher.

If you do this, you will be off to a great start on your journey toward becoming a successful teacher.

2. DO YOUR CHRISTMAS SHOPPING IN THE SUMMER!

While you can't do every aspect of Christmas in the summer, you can certainly do one major component of it—and that is, you can do your Christmas shopping.

Schools are incredibly busy places in December. If you are in elementary or junior/high-middle school, you will typically find December a very short and very intense month. There are fewer teaching days in December than most other months of the school year, and the few teaching days that you have will be constantly interrupted. There are Christmas concert rehearsals and then the Christmas concert itself. This, coupled with decorating the classroom for Christmas, class Christmas parties, and so on, gives December an energy all its own, but at times this energy is not focused on exploring the curriculum.

If you are teaching in a high school, the end of the semester is fast approaching, with final exams, report cards, and semester change. Christmas holidays mean that you have very few teaching days in December, and kids (and perhaps some teachers) can be distracted due to the demands and pressures of the holiday season.

What can you do to take some of the December pressure off of yourself? Get *all* of your Christmas shopping done in the summer, *before* the school

Figure 1.1.

year even begins. As a teacher, you will typically have a great deal of more free time in the summer than you do in December.

If you do decide to do your Christmas shopping in the summer, when December arrives and your colleagues are trying to cope with the demands of school *and* the demands of Christmas, you on the other hand will have taken an enormous amount of stress off of yourself. You will be under a lot less pressure than your colleagues. You may even be able to *enjoy* December at school because you took a great deal of pressure off of yourself by doing your Christmas shopping in the summer.

By the way: There may be some readers who think that they can ignore this tip because they do most or all of their Christmas shopping online. However, even if you do most of your Christmas shopping online, you are still wise to have it all done prior to the start of the school year. Why?

Because even shopping online requires you to make selections, wait for delivery, and wrap gifts once they arrive. And we are all aware that some online sellers take weeks to get their package(s) to you. You can avoid all the stress of wondering if your gift selections are going to arrive on time to get wrapped and ready for Christmas simply by getting all of this done—whether in stores or online—in the summer—well before the school year even begins.

Warning: You may choose to brag to your teaching colleagues in December about how smart you are by having your Christmas shopping already done, but if you do that, please be advised you do so at your own risk!

3. THE STOMACH AND THE BRAIN: HAVE FOOD AVAILABLE FOR YOUR KIDS

The human brain burns about 20 percent of the calories we use each day. The brain needs calories to function properly. This is a fact of nature. Why is this important to you as a teacher?

Because you need to know that *hungry kids do not learn well*. Even if they are trying to focus and learn, their brains will not work well if their brains are calorie starved. (On a side note, neither will yours. Be sure to have a good breakfast—especially on the days when you are teaching.)

Therefore, as a teacher, you always need to have food available in your classroom to give to your hungry kids.

What kind of food works best? While your students may prefer things like chocolate bars or energy drinks, the trouble with these kinds of snacks is that the students who eat these foods will get a sugar spike, followed by a sugar crash. That is not a good thing for learning.

You want to give kids food that will provide them with energy over a longer period of time. Granola bars, trail mix, energy bars, apples, and oranges always work well for most students. Additionally—and this may come as a surprise to you—*popcorn* (minus a lot of salt and butter) is an excellent source of energy, and you can be sure that the majority of your students will love it.

So, when you are setting up your first classroom, be sure to have some place where you can store food to give to your students when they truly need it.

Caution: Never give food to students without first checking to see if they have any food allergies.

And by the way, be careful of the "cons" in your class—the students who will check their lunch and compare it to your snacks and see which of the two they prefer. After all, kids will be kids.

4. VOMIT, COFFEE, AND KETCHUP: HAVE A CHANGE OF CLOTHING AVAILABLE FOR YOURSELF

While classrooms and staffrooms are generally quite unpredictable places, there is one thing that will happen for certain during your teaching career—some student will throw up on you. Or a colleague will spill food or coffee on you (you may even do this to yourself). The odds of this happening are 100 percent, but they go up to 300+ percent if you teach elementary school.

What do you need to do to be prepared for this? *Always* have a *complete* change of clothing available for yourself at school. "Complete" means right down to shoes, socks, and underwear. So when the inevitable happens and you find yourself sprayed with vomit or your top is covered in coffee or ketchup, you will not need to rush home and back; you will not need to arrange coverage for your classes; you will simply change into your spare clothes—the ones you already have at school. Smart!

By the way: Great teachers (especially in elementary school) also have an extra change of clothing available for their students. Typically, it is best to have something generic, for example, sweat pants and a sweat shirt or T-shirt. Little children, especially in the younger grades, will spill things on themselves; some will have accidents and soil themselves. This is very embarrassing, even for a five-year-old. Having clean clothes available that a student can change into quickly will be greatly appreciated. Some teachers even bring a change of clothing for their students along on field trips—because the one thing you can always expect in schools is . . . the unexpected.

Additionally, this does not have to be expensive for you as a teacher. Clothes purchased at used clothing stores work well in cases of emergency. Another strategy that some teachers use is at the end of the school year

Figure 1.2.

(after students have gone home for the summer) they check all of the clothing still left in the lost and found for emergency clothing for their students. There is treasure awaiting in your school's lost and found at the end of each school year.

5. MINTS AND TOOTHPASTE: ESSENTIAL TOOLS FOR EFFECTIVE TEACHING

Some teachers are smokers. Other teachers enjoy spicy foods during their lunch breaks. In either case, this can result in you as a teacher having foul-smelling breath that is less than pleasant for your students to be around as you are trying to teach them.

Early on in my teaching career, I—like some of you—was a smoker. During school hours, I would have a cigarette before school, at lunch, and during my prep periods—anytime I had a break.

Conscious that kids would smell the cigarette smoke on my breath when I went back to class, I would gargle with mouthwash after smoking so as not to have foul-smelling breath if I was working in close proximity with my students when I was back in class.

One day during lunch break, a student came into my office to talk to me (I was an assistant principal at the time as well as teaching—so I had an office). He and I had established a very good relationship. He was the student council president, and I was the student council advisor as well as his teacher.

He told me the following: "I think you should know that some of the kids suspect you are drinking on the job because they have smelled alcohol on your breath. So have I. Some of us wanted to tell you this because we are all a bit worried that you might have a problem and that you might get into trouble and lose your job."

Thank God for honest kids who have your back!

What the kids smelled was my alcohol-based mouthwash.

I pulled out the bottle of mouthwash from my desk drawer, passed it to the student, and asked nicely, "Is this what you smelled?"

"Yup, that's it!" came the reply.

I thanked him and asked him to pass the word around that Mr. Ripley may have problems, but drinking on the job was not one of them.

There are two lessons here for you.

First, when you are working in close proximity with students, you need to smell good. Fresh breath, clean clothes, and deodorant are essential teaching tools.

Second, use only alcohol-free mouthwash at school. Toothpaste and mints work well too, and, unlike alcohol-based mouthwash, they are unlikely to get you into trouble.

So when you are putting together all of the things you will need to set up your classroom, you will need to add mints and toothpaste to your list. Your students will appreciate it.

6. THE BEST TEACHER PREP TOOL EVER MADE: LARGE-CAPACITY FLASH DRIVES

When I moved out of my first school—after having taught there for four years—I had to rent a three-ton truck to haul all of my teaching materials. I had five filing cabinets and twenty-eight tote boxes full of teaching resources—all of it on paper.

Today, I carry a small flash drive around in my wallet. It has enough memory on it to store all of my courses, all of my music, all of my writing, and a great deal more. It could easily store all of the material I took from my first school in those five filing cabinets and twenty-eight tote boxes—with room to spare.

As a teacher—whether you are a preservice teacher, a beginning teacher, or an experienced teacher—you should do yourself a big favor and buy a wallet-sized large-capacity flash drive *now*! You should carry this with you at all times. Why?

Because any time you come across a potentially good teaching resource, you can copy it. You will come across these resources from myriad places, such as other teachers, other students, and online.

Copy everything and anything that you think you might use one day. Save it on your flash drive, on your computer or in the cloud so you can retrieve it at any time in the future that it might prove to be a useful resource for you in your teaching.

Computer memory today is small, cheap, and easy to store.

Start your teaching resources collection *today*!

7. WHO'S THE BOSS? PROBABLY THE PRINCIPAL

Early in your teaching career, there are many unknowns. It is likely that you don't know the curriculum very well, you don't know the resources very well, you don't know your students and their families very well, and you don't know your colleagues and the school administration very well.

So much to learn, so little time!

One of the last things teachers have time to learn are all of the laws, regulations, policies, and contractual obligations that the government, their school board, and their teachers' union have that place expectations and limitations on teacher conduct.

Given this, it is, however, very important that you are aware of one important regulation: the principal is "the boss" of the school—you are not.

Under the terms of your province's or state's School Act, provincial or state regulations, school board policy, and teachers' union collective agreements, the principal has a great deal of authority and decision-making power over the day-to-day running of the school.

It is therefore important for you as a teacher—whether you are in your first year or your twenty-first year of teaching—to learn what authority the principal of your school holds.

If the principal is directing you to do something, you probably ought to do it. If you are in doubt as to whether this directive is appropriate or within the principal's authority, it is best to check with your teachers' union rather than getting into a confrontation with your principal.

So please remember, when it comes to the operation of the school, you're not the boss!

8. WITHOUT THIS, NOTHING ELSE REALLY MATTERS: LESSONS FROM A STUDENT TO A TEACHER

I was asked to set up a high school on a First Nations reserve a few years ago. The director of the school was an old friend. She had been there a year, and the high school was not working well and she thought I might be able to help.

We talked, and I went to "the rez" to take a look.

What I saw were a few kids dropping by the high school when they got bored of doing other things. They were working on self-paced modules, so if they missed a day or several days, they really weren't missing any work—when they decided to show up at school they just picked up where they had left off. And in reality, the work didn't much matter to them anyway.

I agreed to see if we could build something more akin to a "real high school," so I started to teach these kids.

They hated me! Really, there is no other honest way to put it.

In their eyes, I was this "white guy" from the city coming out to "the rez," and I had no business being there and nothing to offer them.

They swore at me—sometimes in English, other times in Cree—sometimes in a whisper, other times loudly.

That was the start of the school year in the fall.

Fast forward to spring: It is a beautiful evening in May of that same year. The school had put on a spring concert that evening, and I was walking around the building after the concert making sure that all the doors were properly shut. A young high school student named Annie was walking with me, chatting about the concert, her friends, school, and so on. It was about 9 o'clock in the evening.

What was this sixteen-year-old indigenous girl doing walking the hallways of the school helping me at 9 o'clock on a beautiful warm spring evening? She was popular and had a lot of friends. Surely she had better things to do.

So I asked, "Annie, why are you here? Your mom and sister have already left. You have lots of other things to do, yet here you are, chatting with me and helping me. Yet, as I recall, when I first started teaching here last fall, *you hated me!* You refused to do any work. You yelled at me in my English class last fall, 'I don't read and I don't write!' What's changed? You and the other kids are so nice to me now. Seriously, I want to know. What happened? Why the change?"

This young lady then proceeded to teach me a lesson that I have never forgotten, one that I believe is at the very heart of what it means to be a good teacher.

"Well Ripley," she replied smiling. "You're right. We did hate you back then. You wanted us to come to school and you made us work when we did. You were pushy and demanding and always wanted more from us."

She continued, "So we made a bet as to how long it would take us to get you to quit. We were mean to you and swore at you and refused to do any work because we figured you would quit—just like all the other 'white guys from the city' who come to the rez."

"But you didn't. You kept coming back. You came every day. You never even took a sick day. Finally, after many months, you just wore us down, and we gave up. We knew that no matter how badly we treated you, you would show up the next day anyway and try to teach us and get us to learn."

At the end of the school year, this same young lady (the one who yelled at me in our first English class, "I don't read and I don't write!" wrote me a beautiful letter about all she had learned that year and what a great experience the year had been for her. I still carry that letter with me to this day.

The lesson that Annie taught me: *Be there!* Make a commitment to your students, and *be there* for them.

Be there when they don't deserve it. *Be there* when they treat you badly. *Be there* when they fight with you because you are trying to get them to do their best and learn something.

Make a commitment to your students to *be there* for them. Let them see and feel and know for certain that you will *be there* for them because you believe they are worth it—even if they don't think they are.

Then even the most challenging students are likely to give you a chance to truly teach them.

By the way #1: While showing up every day is one of the essential elements in developing effective relationships with your students, in and of itself, it is not enough. What you do and how you treat your students *when you show up* matters significantly.

Far too many teachers demand respect from their students, then they turn around and fail to give it back to these very same kids.

It is a great truth about people that all of us want to be treated with *dignity and respect.* I do not mean to imply that you should treat all student *behaviors* with respect. What I am discussing here is treating the *students themselves* with respect.

What does that mean exactly?

Perhaps the best way to approach this question is through a series of questions. Ask yourself the following:

1. Do you genuinely like your students?
2. Do you sincerely care about their success in school (and not just academically, but socially and emotionally as well)?
3. Do you understand how kids in your age/grade level generally behave, and do you make allowances for the fact that kids of the age you are teaching are "not done yet" and therefore they will make mistakes and will not behave appropriately all of the time?
4. Do you *truly* respect the freedom of your students to make choices—even choices that you think are poor?
5. Do you remain kind, welcoming, and supportive to your students, even if they have chosen to misbehave? In other words, do you hold your students accountable for their inappropriate behaviors (which you should), but you do *not* hold a grudge against them after the behavior has been dealt with?

If you can answer "Yes!" to these questions, then you are treating your students respectfully. If you found yourself answering "No!" to some of these questions, it is time for you to do some thinking on this matter.

By the way #2: In the July 2018 issue of *Wired* magazine, Daniel Duane describes his experiences enrolling his daughter at Willie Brown Middle School in San Francisco. This school was "state of the art"—opening in August 2015 at a cost of $54 million. The school had a focus on science, technology, engineering, and math (STEM) and supported this focus with robotics laboratories, Apple TVs in each classroom, and Chromebooks for every student.

Yet, after only one month, the principal had resigned, and there were extensive reports of violence at the school in local media. By October of the first year, the school was on to its third principal, and stories circulated in the community that six teachers had resigned.

What happened? Why had this school, with its beautiful architecture and all of the support it had in terms of modern technology, suffered such an abysmal start?

Eric Hanushek, a professor from Stanford, tells us that of all of the reforms that have been attempted to improve schools over the decades—reforms such as smaller class sizes, more technological support, new buildings, and the like—these all miss something very fundamental to school success. If schools are not staffed with good teachers and good principals—educators who have made a *long-term commitment* to the school and the kids who go there—most of these other reforms are merely window dressing. They look good, but they don't matter much.

Once again, this is the "Annie lesson." If your students (and this applies to a mainly to students who are challenging) do not get a sense from you that you are there for them, and there for the long haul, they will not invest in you. They will not give you the chance to build an effective student-teacher relationship with them, they will not trust you, and they will not respect you.

Great teachers and great school leaders who have made a commitment to their students—nothing can replace that! Fancy furniture and the latest technology are no substitute for competent and committed educators. That is why schools like Willie Brown Middle School fail to live up to expectations—they focus on those things that can be seen and look good, but not nearly enough attention is given to the hearts of the teachers.

9. ESTABLISH A SEATING PLAN THAT ALLOWS MAXIMUM PROXIMITY TO YOUR STUDENTS

One of the first things you will need to do in your classroom is to decide how to arrange the furniture.

This decision will be determined partially based on what kind of furniture is in the room. Do the students sit in desks? At small individual tables? At larger tables? All of these kinds of furniture will present both possibilities and limitations as to how you can arrange your classroom.

Having said that, there are two very important factors you will need to consider in determining how best to arrange how your students will be sitting.

First, you will need to *maximize proximity* to your students. There is a great deal of research (see, e.g., Wehby & Lane, 2009) as well as decades of teaching experience that tells us of this unswerving relationship between student misbehavior and where the teacher is physically in the classroom. It goes like this:

The Proximity Rule: The closer you are to any student or group of students in your classroom, the less likely they are to be off-task or misbehaving.

This is a great truth that all good teachers know and use in their teaching practices and in the ways in which they arrange how students sit in their classrooms.

Second, you will want to configure the students' desks in ways that support the specific kinds of learning activities that you will have them engaged in. Sometimes you will want them in groups of two; other times in groups of four. Still at other times, you may want them working individually.

Many teachers find that the *horseshoe configuration* works very well for them. To do this, you simply place the student desks or tables around the perimeter of the room, and you then direct activities and teach from the center of the horseshoe. This way, you are never more than three steps away from any student.

And lastly, as you teach, *move around the classroom constantly.* Teach from the front, the back, the sides, and the center.

Remember, the closer you are to your students, the more on task they are likely to be.

10. TICK. TICK. TICK.

As we have discussed before, time is a very precious commodity in teaching. *Every moment of every class matters.*

What strategies are you going to use in your classroom to ensure maximum use of the precious little time you have with your students?

One basic and easy strategy that you can implement has to do with *awareness.*

You will find that most classrooms are built with a clock on the wall at the *front* of the room, where the students can easily see it. This positioning, however, is relatively useless for you as a teacher.

What is much more effective for you as a teacher is to place several clocks around the room—*one on each wall.*

The one at the front is for the students, but you should place another large clock on the back wall—with a seconds hand—so that *you* can keep track of where you are in the lesson—how much time has passed and how much time is left.

This is also very useful for giving time-specific tasks during the class, such as "You have five minutes to discuss that in your group and come up with an answer you can all support."

The other reason you will want to place a large clock at the back of the room with a second hand is it will help you with your *wait time.*

There are two kinds of wait time in a classroom.

The first kind of wait time (we will call this "wait time one") is the amount of time that elapses from when you first ask a question of a student or the class and then you begin talking again. For example: "Joe, can you tell me the name of the famous writer we discussed yesterday in class?" If Joe doesn't answer in two seconds and you ask another student after the two seconds have passed, you have a "wait time one" of two seconds.

The second kind of wait time ("wait time two") is the amount of time you are silent *after* a student has responded to your question. To continue from our example above, if Joe answers, "Mark Twain"—how long a period of time elapses *before you react to his answer*? This would be your "wait time two."

In 1972, Mary Budd Rowe published a paper that summarized her research into wait times in classrooms. She had discovered that elementary teachers allow on average only *one second* for a response to a question, and that they follow a student's response with a comment on average within *nine-tenths of a second*. That is not a lot of time.

In 1994, Stahl found:

When students are given 3 or more seconds of undisturbed "wait-time," there are certain positive outcomes:

- The length and correctness of their responses increase.
- The number of their "I don't know" and no answer responses decreases.
- The number of volunteered, appropriate answers by larger numbers of students greatly increases.
- The scores of students on academic achievement tests tend to increase.

When teachers wait patiently in silence for 3 or more seconds at appropriate places, positive changes in their own teacher behaviors also occur:

- Their questioning strategies tend to be more varied and flexible.
- They decrease the quantity and increase the quality and variety of their questions.
- They ask additional questions that require more complex information processing and higher-level thinking on the part of students.

Think about that. All you have to do is *wait three seconds* after asking a question—and learning in your classroom gets substantially better.

But teachers tend to be a bit like TV and radio stations—they hate "dead air," and thus they seem to have this urge to fill the silence.

One way to prevent this is with that clock we talked about—the large clock at the back of the classroom with the seconds hand.

You need to train yourself to *wait at least three seconds* after asking a question; *at least three seconds*—you can wait longer if you want. Watch that large clock on the back wall of your classroom—the one you put there in the summer. Time your *wait times* with it until they come naturally.

The positive effects on both teaching and learning are quite amazing. Seconds do matter!

By the way: While we know that teachers are generally uncomfortable with silence or "dead air" in a classroom after they have asked a question, the same can be said for students. You can use this student discomfort with silence to your advantage. For example, if you find your class reluctant to participate in a class discussion, one strategy you can use to great effect goes like this: Ask your question, and then tell the class you are prepared to wait as long as it takes for a student to answer. Just stand there in silence, looking at the entire class. Do not comment or say anything. You will soon see a hand go up or an answer come your way.

11. THE PROBLEM OF PENS, PENCILS, PAPER . . .

We have all seen this happen in schools many times. A student walks into a classroom and says to the teacher, "I don't have a pen" or "I forgot my notebook" and so on. The student does not have the supplies that are necessary to do the required work. Some teachers get upset at this and spend time chastising the student. This wastes precious class time and often does little or nothing to change the student's behavior.

Effective teachers use a different approach. In setting up their classrooms *before* the beginning of the school year, good teachers set up a *student supply section* somewhere in the classroom. This would be a shelf in the classroom that might have a coffee can filled with pens and paper, a stack of both lined and plain paper, a stapler, a three-hole punch, a roll of tape, and a few copies of any of the textbooks or other kinds of supplies that the students need.

Figure 1.3.

On the *first day of classes*, they tell their students about the routines that are followed in their classrooms. One of these procedures is to tell the students what to do if they came to class without pens, paper, notebooks, and so on. (*Important Note*: You *must* begin the work of establishing routines and procedures—how things will work in your classroom—on the very first class of the year. This is explained in much greater detail in #20.)

What students are instructed to do is to simply go to the "student supply shelf" and take whatever they needed to do their work. There is no need for discussion; there is no need to waste precious class time. Just have your students get what they need and get to work.

This simple strategy is extremely effective. First, let's be honest—we all forget things from time to time. Students are entitled to do this as well, and we should be understanding when this happens to them. Second, no class time whatsoever is wasted discussing what to do about the absence of supplies for a student, because after the first class, they will know what to do and supplies are always available.

By the way: If your school will not supply you with pens and pencils in order for you to implement this strategy, all you need to do is walk down the hallways of your school and over the course of a few days you will be able to collect more than enough pens and pencils. Golf pencils, readily available at any pro shop, work well also.

As for more expensive items like computer notebooks or textbooks, if you want to ensure they get returned, you may want to use this very effective strategy: *have the students leave one shoe on the textbook shelf or with you as collateral for the textbook or notebook*—a shoe which they can happily collect when they return what they borrowed. This strategy works wonderfully, as students seem to always remember to return borrowed items when they get up and start walking with a limp and suddenly remember, "Oh yea, my shoe!"

12. HOW SPONGE ACTIVITIES CAN PREVENT ALL KINDS OF DISCIPLINE ISSUES

"The sponge" has saved countless teachers from all kinds of potential classroom discipline issues.

The role of the sponge in a kitchen is to soak up excess spillage. All teachers will have excess spillage in their classes. This spillage comes in the form of time.

It is rare that you will ever deliver a lesson that ends exactly on time, with all of the students in your class finishing their work at precisely the same moment and at exactly the time the class ends. Never happens!

Instead, what does happen is that some students finish long before other students. Or, you work your way through your lesson plan faster than you thought you would, and there are five or six minutes of class time left when you have finished—not long enough for you to start the next lesson, but more than enough time for your students to get into mischief. What to do?

This is where you should already have "sponge activities" in place for your students. These are activities students can do that "soak up" the extra time they will have on occasion.

Some examples of sponge activities that effective teachers have used for times when individual students finish their work early are:

- Having books like the annual *Guinness Book of World Records* and the annual *Ripley's Believe It or Not!* around the room for the students to browse through. These books are perfect for "sponge time" because students find them colorful, filled with interesting pictures and facts, and very engaging. For younger students, short-story books work well for this, along with a Play-Doh table or drawing table and the like—simple activities that are engaging, fun, and brief.
- Having a wide variety of magazines available, the kind that your students are interested in. For older students, this may range from *Teen Magazine* to *People Magazine* to *Sports Illustrated* to *Car & Driver Magazine* to *National Geographic* to *Fight Magazine*. You need to ask your students near the beginning of the year what kinds of magazines they like (and try not to judge them when they answer). Judging their taste in magazines doesn't help—just get the magazines!

So, before the school year begins, you will want to figure out what you are going to use for "sponge activities" in your classroom. You may want to acquire copies of books and magazines that would be of interest and age-level appropriate for the students you will be teaching. When you set up your classroom in the summer, have these available for your students when school begins, and when you establish your classroom procedures and routines during the first week, teach your kids when and how to use them.

By the way: If you can't afford to subscribe to all of the magazines your kids want, see if you can find friends or colleagues who already subscribe, then ask them to pass along the magazines once they are done with them. Your students generally won't mind reading older editions of something they are interested in.

The point is your students will be reading, they will be engaged in material they are interested in, and they will *not* be getting into mischief.

If your lesson plan finishes early and you find that you have five or ten minutes with the whole class that is free, another option for "sponge time" is to have a computer file prepared with some short, motivational/inspirational video clips that you can show to the entire class.

YouTube, TED Talks, TeacherTube, and so on have many resources that work in situations such as this. Videos about Nick Vujicic, Will Smith motivational videos, the 60 Minutes segment with Eminem about the power of words, Dr. Seuss stories and fairy tales on YouTube for younger kids—all of these work well to soak up the last few minutes of a class. They teach the kids and keep them—*and you*—out of trouble.

13. FACEBOOK, TWITTER, AND TWITS

We live in a digital age where social media is pervasive. Many kids can successfully navigate their way around a touch screen before they are three years old. The parents of your students—and certainly your students—are likely to be very "tech savvy" and have a strong social media presence. Rest assured that when parents/caregivers hear the name of their child's new teacher, many of them will "google you" to see what they discover. So will many of your students. So will prospective employers.

Social media presents several potential pitfalls for teachers.

Wise teachers take a very thorough look at their social media presence—and they do so through the lens of a parent. Ask yourself this question:

Figure 1.4.

"Seeing what you are seeing online about yourself, would you want your child in this teacher's classroom?" It's a fair question.

Those photos you took with your friends on that holiday (you know, the ones in the bar with you chugging beer wearing the "4–20" T-shirt) may have been cool in college or university, but to the parents/caregivers of your students, they may be cause for concern. "Does that teacher have a problem with alcohol? Is that teacher a pot head?" Certain kinds of photos on social media give rise to those kinds of questions.

Smart teachers "sanitize" their digital presence (Facebook, Twitter, Instagram, Pinterest, etc.) to project a very safe and professional look. This will help you get and keep a teaching job and will also alleviate potential concerns from parents/caregivers.

If you already have a teaching position, another problem may arise. With older students and some parents, you may find yourself getting "friend requests" on your Facebook page.

Never accept such requests.

You are a teacher 24/7/365. You are held—by virtue of being a teacher—to a high standard of conduct and are under more public scrutiny than the plumber or the accountant who lives next door.

Do yourself a favor and keep what privacy you can. And keep the parents/caregivers and your students at a professional distance. You are a teacher—not their Facebook friend. If you need more friends, find them elsewhere—but not among your students or their caregivers.

14. THE ONLY THREE WAYS TO TEACH A CHILD

There are only three ways to teach a child. The first is by example, the second is by example, the third is by example.

—Albert Schweitzer

Many teachers are by nature keen observers of human behavior. One of the great truths of teaching gleaned from such observations is: *we teach who we are*. This manifests itself in many ways in teaching, but two are foremost.

First, think about the subject(s) you chose to study in your preservice teacher education or the subjects you are teaching now (assuming you had some degree of choice in this). Why are you teaching chemistry and not social studies? Why are you teaching elementary students and not teenagers?

The subjects we choose to teach and the age level of the students we choose to teach say a great deal about who we are.

Most often we have studied these particular subjects because we like them; we are drawn to them; they matter to us. That tells us something about who we are.

The age level of the students we choose to teach is equally informative. For example, you may prefer teaching younger students to older students. There is nothing wrong with teaching either, but your preferences here can give you much insight into who you are if you spend some time reflecting on *why* you have these preferences. Are you afraid of the older students—afraid that you might not be able to handle them? Are you concerned that the older students will challenge your knowledge of the subjects you are teaching—and you lack both knowledge and confidence in this regard? These are questions worth exploring.

The second aspect of teacher identity that shows itself in our classrooms is in the area of curriculum.

Many teachers believe that what they are teaching is the curriculum. By this, they typically mean the authorized curriculum or Program of Studies that is approved by their state or province.

But there is another curriculum alive and well in every classroom in every school—the "hidden curriculum."

The hidden curriculum refers to the things that teachers convey to their students *unintentionally and/or indirectly.* Teachers do this through their actions, their beliefs, and what they value in the classroom.

For example, if teachers start and end virtually every class on time, they are communicating that punctuality matters and that teaching time is precious. They may never overtly teach this, or they may never say the words, but their actions certainly convey this message to their students.

The same applies to myriad other aspects of the lived daily life of the classroom—from how the teacher treats their students (kind, strict, bully?) and the methods the teacher uses to instruct (didactic, teacher-controlled, student-centered, project-based, inquiry, all of these?) to the way in which the desks or tables are arranged and who decides where students get to sit. All of these teacher behaviors send messages to the students.

And just how does a teacher arrive at what they think are the "best" answers to these kinds of questions for themselves?

Many teachers teach the way they were taught. Through the "apprenticeship of observation" (Lortie, 1975) and by what they saw their teachers do when they were students, many teachers come to believe that they have "learned" how to teach. They are drawn to what is familiar—the ways they were taught when they were in school.

In addition to this, we all have personal preferences and biases. For example, there are teachers who played a lot of sports growing up, and perhaps still do. Because of this, they will likely have a certain partiality for kids who are athletic and involved in sports.

Growing up as a child, the biggest "sin" a child could commit in my house was to be lazy. It was absolutely and at all times unacceptable. Thus, as a teacher, I have a strong preference for kids who work hard over kids who are naturally smart and who perform well but tend to be lazy.

A teacher may be completely unaware of the preferences and biases they have; nonetheless, these biases will certainly have an impact on the teacher's relationships with their students. However, the problem is this teacher won't even know it.

As teachers, we need to be very careful about our biases and the "hidden curriculum" we are teaching in our classrooms. The problem with this is that it is all too often hidden from us as teachers, but it is not hidden from our students whatsoever. To them, these biases are abundantly clear.

It is the wise and effective teacher who spends some time examining their preferences and prejudices and how they might manifest in their classroom. If you bring these into the light, then—and only then—can you manage them in ways that positively impact teaching and learning in your classroom.

Remember, *we teach who we are*. So if you want your students to be punctual, you need to be punctual. If you want your students to work hard, you need to work hard. If you want your students to be honest, you need to be honest with them. If you want your students to be kind, you need to be kind. A good example is far more effective than words can ever be.

> No written work, no spoken plea,
> can teach our youth what they should be.
> Nor all the books on all the shelves,
> it's what the teachers are themselves.
> (Wooden, 1997, *Wooden:*
> *A Lifetime of Observations and*
> *Reflections on and off the Court*)

By the way: One of the qualities of great teachers is that they are lifelong learners. They are curious by nature and tend to want to improve themselves on an ongoing basis, both personally and professionally. Thus, some tend to read a great deal; others take courses; others learn how to play an instrument, or they learn a new hobby.

Doing this can help you relate with greater empathy to the students in your classes. When you attempt to learn something that does not come easily to you, it can help you understand the frustrations and disappointments some of your students feel when they struggle to learn what you are trying to teach.

I began taking piano lessons when I was in my forties. I was terrible. I had to work very hard just to be mediocre. It was an excellent lesson in empathy for me. It helped me remember that for some of my students, learning what I was trying to teach them did not come easy. We all need to remember this. It helps us with empathy, and it helps us with patience.

15. NO MATTER WHERE YOU GO, THERE YOU ARE

Confucius said: "No matter where you go, there you are."

In #14, it was argued that we teach who we are. If this is so (and it is), then it is obviously important that as teachers, we have a good understanding of who we really are.

If you want to know who you are, it is equally important to know *who you've been*. Your background in life will have a significant impact on who you are as a teacher and how you relate to your students.

This truth was made very clear to me a few years ago when I was working with a first-year teacher.

We were teaching in a Grade 7 to 9 school, which could be described in general terms as being very diverse in terms of its student population. There were a few kids from affluent homes, a lot of kids from more middle-class homes, and a significant number of kids who came from homes that could accurately be described as "working poor."

This young teacher was bright and hardworking and genuinely cared about the kids and the quality of her teaching. She had been an A+ student all of her life, and she placed a high value on education.

Yet, she was having significant discipline issues in all of her classes—and this was early in the school year.

I also taught some of these same classes, so I knew these students well. I wasn't having any problems with these kids, nor were most of their other teachers, so I concluded the problem likely wasn't the kids.

Clearly, there was something going on with her teaching and her relationship with her students.

I decided that if I was going to help her, I needed to see her classes in action. I told the kids ahead of my observation that they were to ignore my presence in her room and that they wouldn't get into any trouble from me for misbehaving (unless someone ended up bleeding). They laughed and agreed to behave as they normally did in this teacher's room.

What I observed came as a shock to me. These kids—*my* kids, kids who were polite and respectful and hardworking and fun to teach in my classroom—had transformed into little monsters in her classroom. They were defiant, disrespectful, disruptive, and off-task for virtually the entire class.

This young teacher kept droning on at the front of the room, clearly embarrassed, clearly not in control, and clearly with no one listening to her.

When we met later that day to discuss what happened, she broke down and cried. I asked her how long things had been this way, and she said it started sometime during the first week of school.

I inquired about that first week, what she had done to begin to establish a good working relationship with the kids, what she had done to establish effective classroom procedures, and what teaching methods she had used.

She looked at me in disbelief. "Why should I have to do any of those things?" she replied. "I'm the teacher—they're the students. I know the content—they don't. They're supposed to listen to me and take notes and study for the tests and do what I tell them to do. That's what I did when I was a student—when I was their age—and they should be doing the same things now!"

Ahhhhh! There it was!

She believed (this A+ student all of her life) that her students should behave just like she did when she was their age. She believed that the teacher should have *automatic legitimacy* simply because he or she was the teacher.

The kids, however, had a different point of view—and so did I.

This young lady might have been a reasonably effective teacher if she was teaching in a highly academic school where all of the students needed to pass her course to move on to the next level. However, this was not the nature of these students at all.

She quit a week later, and for the sake of the students, I was relieved.

If, when you were young, you had been a "street kid"—tough, street smart, a survivor—you will likely relate well to those kinds of kids when you become their teacher. Having said that, these kinds of students would present a much greater challenge for a teacher who had come from an upbringing where education was valued, homework was always done, and the teacher was always right.

Remember this, and be cautious of its implications in your classroom: *We like kids who like us—and we really like kids who are a lot like us.*

While this is both true and understandable, it can cause a lot of problems for you as a teacher if you fail to find ways to work with students who are not like you at all.

There is a Chinese proverb that says: "We see what is behind our eyes."

Our backgrounds and previous experiences have a substantial impact on how we interpret and respond to our current experiences.

As a teacher, you need to be very aware of the filters through which you are seeing your students and do whatever you can to ensure that these filters are helping—not hindering—your work with them.

16. IS TEACHING REALLY YOUR GIFT?

A quote often attributed to Pablo Picasso is as follows: "The meaning of life is to find your gift. The purpose of life is to give it away."

This leads us to a question of extreme significance for anyone beginning or continuing a career in education: *Is teaching your gift?*

What do we mean by "gift" in this sense?

In his book *Let Your Life Speak: Listening for the Voice of Vocation*, Parker Palmer (2000) discusses the answer to this question from the perspective of *vocation*. He argues that some people go into teaching as a job, others as a career, but only those who have a vocation to teach should actually become teachers.

Palmer describes vocation this way:

> Vocation does not come from willfulness. It comes from listening. I must listen to my life and try to understand what it is truly about—quite apart from what I would like it to be about—or my life will never represent anything real in the world, no matter how earnest my intentions. That insight is hidden in the word *vocation* itself, which is rooted in the Latin for "voice." Vocation does not mean a goal that I pursue. It means a calling that I hear. Before I can tell my life what I want to do with it, I must listen to my life telling me who I am. I must listen for the truths and values at the heart of my own identity, not the standards by which I must live—but the standards by which I cannot help but live if I am living my own life.
>
> (pp. 4–5)

So the question you must ask—then answer in depth, truthfulness, and complete honesty—is this: *Did you hear that call to be a teacher? Is teaching truly your gift, and are you being called to give your gift away?*

In *When Breath Becomes Air* neurosurgeon Paul Kalanithi (2016) states: "Putting lifestyle first is how you find a job—not a calling." He is not wrong, and this truly applies to teaching (p. 69).

Are you looking for a job, or are you answering a call? Is it the lifestyle of teaching that appeals to you—the familiarity of school, the hours, the vacation time, the job security, the pension—or is it something that you must do because it is who you are?

For your sake, and the sake of all of the children you teach or may come to teach, you need to discover the answer to this question: Are you *really* called to be a teacher?

Some people hear this calling years before they actually become teachers. Others hear it when they do their student teaching and find that they are really good at teaching and find it fulfilling. Still others hear this call sometime early in their actual teaching careers. The point is if you have been teaching for a while and find it to be a job (and not a very pleasant job at that) then you

Figure 1.5.

really ought to find some other line of work. To stay in teaching feeling like that is to do great damage—both to your students and to yourself.

And please reflect on this: just because you love children does not mean you are called to be a teacher. Perhaps you are called to be a parent, or a social worker, or a daycare provider. Teaching does *not* require that you want to teach and care for children—it requires that you teach and care for *other peoples' children.*

17. HALF STEP, FULL STEP, STEP AND A HALF: HOW MANY STEPS WILL YOUR KIDS BE TAKING WITH YOU THIS YEAR?

In *What the Dog Saw*, Malcolm Gladwell (2009) discusses the work of Eric Hanushek from Stanford University. Hanushek states that there have been a number of studies conducted that clearly show how much impact an effective teacher can make on student outcomes.

Hanushek goes on to state:

> In one study of mine, teachers near the top of the quality distribution got an *entire year's worth of additional learning* out of their students compared to those near the bottom. That is, *a good teacher will get a gain of 1.5 grade level equivalents while a bad teacher will get 0.5 year during a single academic year.* Importantly, this analysis considered kids just from minority and poor inner-city families, indicating that family background is not fate and that good teachers can overcome deficits that might come from poorer learning conditions in the home. (Emphasis added)
>
> (Hanushek, 2014)

If you want to get a good sense of what this really means, have two students or two colleagues line up with their backs against the door or a wall of your classroom.

Have one student take a half step forward, which represents half of a school year (this student had a weak teacher) and have the other student take a step and a half forward, which represents a year and a half of a school year (this student had a great teacher). That's Grade 1. At the end of Grade 1, our first student (the one with the weak teacher) is only half way through the Grade 1 curriculum, while the other student (the one with the great teacher) is now performing at the middle of Grade 2 level.

Continue this for all six years of elementary school, and then take a good look at the gap between these two students.

According to Hanushek's research, after six years of schooling, a student who had poor-performing teachers for all six years would be performing at a Grade 3 level. The student with great teachers for all six years would be performing at a Grade 9 level—*a full six years difference.*

And remember, Hanushek's work was done with minority and poor inner-city families, where a significant number of the kids came from homes that were not or could not be very supportive of the efforts of their teachers.

So please remember: *the quality of your teaching will make an enormous difference in the lives of your students, no matter what their home situation is like. Yes, you* can *make a difference—a very significant difference.*

Never, never, never forget that!

Section Two

What You Need to Do with Your Students on the First Day and during the First Week of School

INTRODUCTION

It is impossible to understate the importance of the first day and the first week of your school year as a teacher. The impressions you make, the expectations you set, the procedures you establish, and the boundaries you create will all set the stage for your success—or lack thereof—for the rest of the school year.

And there are no "do overs"—you quite simply will not get a second chance to do your first day and your first week over again until the next September, so it is critical that you get it right the first time.

That is what this section is about—getting your first day and your first week right—the first time you do it.

18. YOU NEVER GET A SECOND CHANCE TO MAKE A FIRST IMPRESSION

In the 1980s, a shampoo company made a commercial to sell an anti-dandruff shampoo in which the tag line was: "You never get a second chance to make a first impression."

Clever writing and a great lesson for all teachers.

Think about the first time you will meet, or did meet, the rest of the school staff (which is usually a week or two before school starts). Think about the first time you will meet, or did meet, your students on the first day of school. Think about your first parent-teacher open house in the fall, where parents are introduced to the staff.

On all of these occasions, you are the *new teacher* (an experience you will have every time you move schools throughout your career). As such, the students, the staff, and the parents will all be "checking you out." The way you dress, the way you talk, your energy, and your demeanor will all make a "first impression"—an impression that will set the stage for what comes after.

Because first impressions are so important for a teacher, you need to be very mindful of the kind of first impression you want to make.

I always dressed well for teaching—mostly business casual. I was once teaching in a high school with a student population that many would describe as rough, tough, disinterested, and defiant.

After a couple of months there, one student asked me openly in class, "Why do you dress up to come here? None of the other teachers dresses up."

I replied, "Well, I do it for you. I do it to show respect for you and for the work we do here, because I think you are important and I think what we do here is important."

There was no response, just a few very puzzled looks by the students.

Things changed a bit after that conversation in my classroom—they got somewhat better. Most of these students had never thought of themselves as "important" before.

How you *look* during all of these "firsts" is extremely significant. In his book *Blink: The Power of Thinking without Thinking*, Malcolm Gladwell (2005) tells us that we all make snap judgments in all parts of our lives, primarily based on past experience.

Daniel Kahneman (2011) makes a similar argument in *Thinking Fast and Slow*. Kahneman demonstrates that many of us make decisions based on the WYSIATI premise (What You See Is All There Is). We often make quick judgments and snap decisions based on very partial and incomplete information, thinking that "what we see is all there is to see"—and this is especially true when we meet new people. We judge their gender, their clothes, their overall appearance, and their looks—and this judging starts within milliseconds of our seeing them for the first time.

As *the new teacher* (whether it is your first teaching position or you are an experienced teacher who has moved to a new to a school), all of the people you meet—staff, students, parents—will be making judgments about you (as you too will be judging them), and much of this will be taking place at the subconscious level.

Thus, you need to consciously ask yourself, "Exactly what kind of first impression do you want to make—and how are you going to go about making it?"

First, it is extremely prudent for you to dress as the professional you are. People will judge you at first on how you look. Additionally, if you are in the early stages of your career and may thus be among the youngest of your peers and where you may be younger than the parents/caregivers of the children you teach, you will have this age gap to contend with. You can partially overcome the tendency that some staff and some parents/caregivers may have to "look down on you because you are so young" by dressing professionally.

Don't worry about how the more-experienced or older teachers dress. They may be able to pull off a more casual look because they have earned a certain respect and deference over the years. You may not be there yet. You need to act professionally, and this starts by dressing professionally.

Additionally, you also need to think about the kind of first impression that your classroom gives as well. How do you want your classroom to *feel* in regard to openness, friendliness, warmth, and learning? Give a great deal of thought to this as it is of critical importance. Will you do all of the decorating, or will you get some kids to help? Will you seek advice from veteran teachers as to how best to set up your room, or will you "go it alone"? Will there be spaces on your walls that the students "own" and where they choose what gets put up on their spaces, or will the bulletin boards be controlled solely by you?

Keep all of this in mind, and proceed accordingly, all the while knowing: "You never get a second chance to make a first impression!"

19. PIZZA AND MOVIES: THE BEST INVESTMENTS YOU MAY EVER MAKE

Never forget that at its essence, teaching is about relationships. Kids don't learn well from teachers they don't like (see Rita Pierson's TED Talk [2013] on this—it is well worth eight minutes of your time). Effective teaching can happen only over the long haul when your students like and respect you, when you have established a good working relationship with them based on mutual trust and respect. That is simply a given in teaching.

However, this leads to the question, "How do you go about building such relationships with your students, especially in a school where you are a new teacher with no history with your students?"

One strategy that can be used effectively with upper elementary to high school students is to find out from other teachers which students are the leaders in your upcoming class—the class you are going to teach next fall. Which students have influence over their peers? These students may been seen as "positive" leaders, or as "negative" leaders—but either way, they have influence, and you need them on your side as quickly as possible if you are going to be successful in teaching that particular class. The onus is on you—not them—to begin the work of building an effective working relationship.

Then, every summer before school starts, invite these student leaders to come to school for a few days to help you set up the classroom. This means doing things like decorating bulletin boards, putting books in shelves, figuring out how you want to arrange the furniture, and so on.

Now, most kids have better things to do in the last weeks of summer vacation than to come in to school to help the new teacher—someone they don't even know. You have to lure them.

It is really quite amazing how much work you can get out of kids with payment of pizzas or movie certificates. Some of the more capitalistic kids will only work for cash—and that's OK as well. You need them on board more than they need you at that stage.

Figure 2.1.

As they work on getting the classroom ready, you can choose to help them, or you can do your own work at your desk, listening discreetly to their conversations with one another.

It is amazing the kinds of valuable insights into their friends, families, interests as well as their views of school, life, and the future that you can glean in situations such as this, insights that can prove invaluable to you throughout the school year.

Additionally, it is wise to designate some of the spaces in the classroom as "student spaces"—bulletin boards or areas where these student leaders can put up any kinds of displays they want (within the bounds of what is reasonable, of course).

These student spaces typically become sacrosanct. They are rarely tampered with, even where the student population is most challenging. Other students usually do not dare put graffiti on these displays because the student leaders created them and there will be consequences from them if their displays are damaged.

This kind of activity helps you to teach your students a lesson that you need them to learn if you are going to work together successfully for the rest of the year. This is not *your* classroom; this is *our* classroom.

When you do this, these student leaders have a voice in how their classroom looks and how it is going to function. Through this, you have established a degree of ownership on their part, and we all know we take care of what we see as *ours* typically better than what we see as *yours*.

Another thing that can be accomplished during these "classroom setup days" is that these student leaders and you can begin to bond a little. They can get to know you in a small way as the person you are outside of a more formal "teacher in the classroom" role, and you get to know them a little as persons, not simply as students.

20. WHY PROCEDURES AND ROUTINES—THE WAY WE DO THINGS IN OUR CLASSROOM—ARE CRITICAL TO SUCCESSFUL TEACHING

In the introduction to section 1, we described the "magic" of a master teacher's classroom, the kind of classroom that you may have been lucky enough to observe as a student or in your student teaching where things just *flowed*. The teacher asked the kids to do something, and the kids just did it. The teacher moved from teaching science to teaching math, and the transition between subjects went quickly and smoothly.

This, of course, begs the question: *How* did these teachers get their students to be so cooperative? *How* did these teachers decide what routines to use, for what aspects of classroom practice, and *how* did they get their students to follow these procedures?

The simple answer is: *On the first day of school and during the first week of school and all through the first month of school, these teachers established very clear classroom procedures that evolved into classroom routines.*

It is important for you to know why the establishing of classroom procedures is absolutely fundamental to successful teaching.

Think about all of the following events that will occur in your classroom over and over again throughout the school year:

1. Students will enter and exit the classroom.
2. Students will hand in homework assignments or hand in exams.
3. Students will come to class without their homework completed.
4. Students will transition from one subject to another or from one activity to another.
5. Students will have questions they want to ask you, or comments they want to make.
6. Students will come to class late or want to leave early.
7. Students will want to go to the washroom.
8. Students will come to class without the necessary supplies.
9. Students will finish their work before the allotted time is up.
10. You will want to take attendance.
11. You will want to have the class stop what they are doing and pay attention to you.
12. You will want students to stop one activity and move on to something else.
13. You will want to distribute learning materials to the students.
14. You will want students to catch up on missed work if they were away.

This list is made up of those classroom events that happen virtually on a daily basis. This list, however, is by no means complete. For example, some students will (especially in the higher grades) want to appeal their marks at certain times. On occasion, some students will be absent for exams and will want to know how to make up for the missed exam mark. However, these are fairly exceptional (although you will still need to have procedures in place for dealing with these events as well).

Because of the frequent nature of the behaviors on this list, it is of crucial importance that you teach your students *how* to perform these procedures the way that *you* want them performed in your classroom—*beginning with your very first class*—and that you *practice these procedures* until your students know how to do them properly.

You need to understand that any student who has not had you as a teacher before has no idea of how these things work in *your* classroom. They will be wondering where to sit, what are the classroom rules, what happens if they are late, how do they ask and answer questions in your classroom, and so on.

These are fair questions, and you need to have a strategy in place that answers these questions for *your* students in *your* classroom.

It is of critical importance that you understand this: *Your students don't decide how these procedures work in your classroom;* you do!

Let us begin with a simple example. How do you want your students to enter your classroom, and where do they go once there are in your room?

CAUTION: Do not assume that your students know how to do this in *your* classroom, because different teachers have different expectations and procedures as to how they want their students to do this. Therefore, you cannot expect your students to know what *your* expectations are unless you: (1) *tell* them what your expectation are; (2) *show* them what your expectations are; and (3) *practice* what your expectations are.

Remember the three steps: (1) tell; (2) show; and (3) practice.

Here is an upper elementary or junior/high-middle school example of this notion of establishing a routine of how to enter a classroom following these three steps.

On the first day of school, your students have no idea what your expectations are in regard to how you want them to enter your classroom or what to do once they are inside. How can they? You haven't taught them this procedure yet.

Given this fact, what you need to do with your students before the school year starts is first establish a seating plan. You may decide to let them sit wherever they choose, or you may assign them desks according to a predetermined seating plan. In either case, you need to determine where students are going to sit in your classroom once school begins.

On the first day of school, after all of the students enter your classroom (usually in a rather chaotic and random way), you should ask all of the students to follow you out into the hallway. There, tell them *in very specific detail* what your expectations are for how they are to enter the classroom and what they are to do once they are inside. This usually takes the form of the teacher *telling* them, "You need to enter our classroom quietly—talking to your friends is fine but you must use your inside voice—and then you make your way *directly* to your desk and sit down and get your materials out so you are ready for learning. Three steps: (1) Enter quietly. (2) Go directly to your desk. (3) Get your supplies out and get ready to learn."

You may want to repeat these instructions at least twice, and ask if anyone needs you to *show* them how to do this (usually there were no takers as these three steps are pretty simple).

Next, tell them we were going to *practice* doing this, and once they get it right, we can begin the class.

At this point, have the students enter the classroom—now for the second time, but *this time knowing your expectations*. If they do so in an acceptable manner, you can begin to teach the class (although in actuality, you already began teaching them—you taught them how to enter your classroom, and that you as a teacher have clear expectations about student behaviors). If they didn't do this properly, you can go back into the hallway, review your procedures, and practice it again (although this is rarely necessary).

Establishing classroom routines and procedures for *your* classroom (the way things are done in *your* classroom) is important at any level, from kindergarten to Grade 12. Do not skip this step at the very beginning of the school year, no matter what grade level you are teaching.

By the way #1: Every once in a while, you will get a student who simply doesn't want to follow your procedures; one student who—even after the rest of the class choses to enter your classroom properly—still insists on being loud and/or wandering around. What can you do in a case like this? This strategy has been proven to be very effective if you ever have one or a few students who are unwilling to follow this procedure.

In the example of learning how to enter your classroom, you simply ask the student this question: "How many times will it take you—*after school today*—to enter and exit our classroom until you can show me that you have learned how to do it properly?" Most often, students quickly reply, "Once!" You then meet the student after school; the student (who is now by themselves, with no audience to entertain) enters your classroom according to your procedures and is then sent on his or her way.

Here is another example of a way you can establish a classroom procedure, this time with older students.

What procedure will you establish in your classroom for students to follow when they must hand in assignments and exams? Elementary teachers often use a box or basket for this purpose. For older students, however, this can be a problem when the students' paper goes "missing" and they claim to have handed it in. For older students, a procedure that works well goes like this: tell your students that their exams and their assignments were very precious to you. As their teacher, you expected them to work hard and do their best; therefore you owe them the respect of taking great care of these tests and assignment once they handed them in to you.

And *handed in* was what you insist on—quite literally. When students are turning in an exam or assignment to you, you instruct them to place it *directly into your hands—in front of at least one other student*. That way, you can tell them if you ever lost their work, the onus is now on you. The students have a least one witness who can say that they had handed in their assignment or exam, and once it is literally in your hands, the responsibility for the "chain of custody" of their work had clearly passed from them to you.

By establishing this procedure for handing in exams and assignments, you can avoid the issue of students telling you that they left their exam on your desk or that they had slipped their assignment under your classroom door, and then attempting to blame you for losing their work. That will *not* be your procedure for handing in exams and assignments. Problem solved!

Question: What is the difference between a *procedure* and a *routine*?

You establish procedures for all of the day-to-day activities that will take place repeatedly in your classroom throughout the school year. There are fourteen of these in the list provided in this strategy. You *tell, show*, and *practice* these procedures—beginning on the first day of school, and throughout the first month of school—until they become the *routines* in your classroom.

Your *procedures* become *routines* when your students do them *automatically*, without having to be told what to do. And that is one of the traits of all master teachers, that is, what you saw if you were fortunate enough to see a master teacher in action during your school years or during your student teaching experiences. That is why the classroom just seemed to *flow*—it was *because the teacher had spent time at the start of the year establishing procedures* for all of the day-to-day events of the classroom, and *these procedures became classroom routines.*

The establishment of procedures and routines does not happen automatically in any classroom. It takes planning, execution, and practice early in the school year. It is extremely important that you as the teacher are *consistent* in the routines you establish. You *must be sure to follow your routines consistently*; otherwise students will get confused and will be unsure as to whether or not you really mean what you say in this regard.

As well, there may be occasions when as a teacher you need to remind your students of what these procedures are. You may even have to practice these from time to time throughout the school year.

However, the payoff is incredible. *You will save hours of valuable teaching time each year.* You will avoid having confused students who are unclear about how to do these things in your classroom. And you will avoid numerous confrontations with students who want to do things their own way because you have established very early and very clearly in the school year how things work in your classroom.

This is effective class management—the procedures and routines that you establish early in the school year with your students that will optimize both the quality and quantity of teaching and learning time in your classroom.

By the way #2: Class management and *student discipline* are *not* the same things. As stated above (and this does bear repeating) *class management* refers to the routines and procedures that you establish early in the school year with your entire class that will optimize both the quality and quantity of teaching and learning time in your classroom.

Student discipline is your *response* and the *consequences* that you provide to a student or a group of students who disrupt or interfere with the learning environment that you have established in your classroom or the school. These consequences must be clearly spelled out in advance, and *they must be nonnegotiable.*

When you let students know—*in advance*—what the consequences will be if they choose to behave inappropriately, you are empowering your students to make *informed choices.* If they then choose to behave inappropriately, by doing so they have chosen to accept the consequences—consequences they knew would be required of them because you informed them of these in advance and you *always* follow through on what you say you will do.

In such circumstances, there is really no need to get mad at a student who makes this kind of choice. Instead, *please respect their freedom to choose.* They made a choice, they accept the consequences (whether they like the consequences or not is really quite irrelevant), and once these consequences have been carried through, all you need to say is, "Welcome back!"

Kids flourish in an environment such as this. They know exactly what is expected of them. They know exactly what will happen if they choose to comply or if they choose to not comply. And they know that with absolute certainty, you will hold them accountable for their choices.

By the way #3: Rules! You have probably seen teachers who have a long list of "Classroom Rules" posted somewhere in their room. This is usually *not* a good sign.

In effective classrooms, there are generally only one or two rules (sometimes posted; sometimes not). A rule such as "Be respectful of everyone in this class" covers a lot of ground. It includes behaviors such as don't lie; don't interfere with teaching and learning; don't take what is not yours; and so on.

Give kids freedom—but within very strict boundaries that are nonnegotiable.

For example, I would tell my high school students, "You can sleep in my class if you need to, because then you are only interfering with *your* learning and *your* success at school. However, should you snore, I will have to wake you up very abruptly by kicking the legs of your chair (after "maybe" telling the rest of the class to get out their phones because this could be really funny) because your snoring is interfering with both *my teaching* and your *classmates learning.*"

Oddly, I never had a student sleep in my class. I like to think it was because I was so engaging as a teacher and the material we were exploring was so relevant to the students. But, perhaps, it might have been the fear of a YouTube upload. In either case, sleeping in class was a non issue.

As all great teachers know, when you manage your classroom well, discipline problems become very, very rare.

By the way #4: Humor is a teacher's secret weapon. You can use it to build relationships. You can use it to prevent or diffuse potential discipline situations. It is a wonderful tool to have in your "teacher toolbox."

Some teachers use sarcasm and call it humor. It is not! Belittling students with sarcasm does nothing to build an effective teacher-student relationship; it only damages it.

So figure out what makes your students laugh, what makes you laugh, and then have some fun with your kids.

I have gone to many concerts and shows in my years of teaching—where I paid more than $100 for my ticket—and these performers were not nearly as entertaining or as funny as most of the classes that I had taught that day. One sign that you are successful as a teacher is this: your classroom is a place of joy and laughter, a place where the difference between work and play is difficult to discern.

21. START TEACHING THE CURRICULUM ON DAY 1

If you followed the previous suggestions, you have your students inside your classroom, seated at their assigned desks or tables, ready to learn. While you may want to spend some time during that first class going over other procedures for your classroom (and this is certainly something you will likely want to do), one thing you *must* do during that first class is *get your students working on curriculum.*

Teaching time is precious. One of the most common laments of teachers is, "There is never enough time!" Never enough time to do all of the things you want. Never enough time to complete all of the objectives in the curriculum. Yet, at the same time, many teachers waste a great deal of time in their classroom. Please do not be one of those teachers.

Your students need to know that they are there to learn and you are there to teach. They need to know—right away, the very first class—that you believe what you have to teach is important, that their learning what you have to teach is important, and that we all need to get to work as quickly as possible because time is precious and the clock is ticking and that "all too soon . . . it will be June."

Remember, you have two priorities on the first day of school. Your first priority is to begin to teach your students the procedures they need to know in order to begin work in your classroom. Other procedures, like handing in assignments and what they are to do when they have missed work, can wait until later on in the first week.

Your second priority is to get your students working on the curriculum. Some teachers use an activity called the "Newspaper of the Self," which is explained in the next strategy. It is something that your students can do right away, it is interesting to most of them, and it provides you as the teacher with invaluable information about each of your students.

No matter what it is you choose to have your students do, get them working on curriculum as quickly as possible. It sets a great precedent for what they can expect in your classroom for the rest of the year.

22. TO KNOW THEM IS TO LOVE THEM . . . WELL, MOST OF THE TIME

In #19, we discussed one way to attempt to begin to build a good working relationship with student leaders in your class. But what about the rest of the kids? How do you learn about them and how to best work with them?

One strategy that has been used for decades that teachers have found to be very effective was to do some kind of activity in the first week of school (some teachers start with this on the first day) that enables you to get to know all of your students better. One such activity is the "Newspaper of the Self."

It works like this. Tell your students that they are going to write a small newspaper. This newspaper is to be similar to a typical daily newspaper in that it will have a current events section, a sports section, an entertainment section, a travel section, a business section, and so on.

However, the difference is that in each of these sections, your students will be writing about themselves.

For example, in the sports section, they would write about the sports they liked to play or watch. If they don't like sports, they can write about why they feel this way. In the entertainment section, they will write about their favorite TV shows, favorite music, favorite stars, and favorite movies. In the travel section, they will write about their favorite trip (and this does not have to be a big trip, as in travel out of the country—it could be a "trip" that was in the neighborhood or within the city where we were located).

When you read and assess these Newspapers of the Self, it will enable you to learn about each student's interests and activities, as well as their writing abilities and work ethic. You can then use examples and metaphors in your teaching from the music and TV and movies that your students are familiar with. This is a great teaching tool, and an effective way to get certain concepts across to your students.

As well, the information you gather from this assignment can provide you with invaluable information that you can use to help start building a relationship with your students.

If you learn that Cory loves skateboarding, you can chat with him about that. If you learn that Jamie is into basketball and the NBA in a big way, you can talk to her about that. If you learn that Sam loves *South Park* and *The Simpsons* . . . well, you get the idea.

This start of the school year project helps to get your students thinking and writing immediately, and it has the spin-off benefit of helping you to build connections early in the year—the beginnings of an effective student-teacher relationship.

As a teacher, you really need to first *learn about your students as people* before you can begin to build an effective teacher-student relationship with them.

And once you do, you will probably find that besides learning about them, you also may learn to like them . . . well, most of them anyway.

23. WHY SHOULD THE KIDS LISTEN TO YOU? THE IMPORTANCE OF ESTABLISHING LEGITIMACY

In *The Hidden Curriculum Revisited* (Feinberg, Walter, & Soltis, 1992), Paul Willis tells the story of a group of boys he nicknames "the lads." The lads live in a factory town. Their grandfathers and their fathers have all worked at the local factory.

These boys are constantly getting into trouble at school because they see their future as working in the factory, like their fathers and grandfathers before them. They do not see the knowledge being explored in the classroom as having any relevance for them whatsoever.

What is happening here is that *their teacher has failed to establish legitimacy*. Their teacher has failed to show these boys that the work they are doing in the classroom each day is directly related to and important to their lives—now and in the future.

Thus, the lads don't care about class content—why should they? Therefore, they spend their time and energy on what they do care about—making the other kids laugh and getting themselves out of work.

Willis puts it this way:

> The teacher's authority must be won and maintained on moral, not on coercive grounds. *There must be consent from the taught.* This moral authority is cemented for most students when they accept the basic exchange that the teachers offer them in various ways. The bargain is struck along the following lines. If the students give the teachers respect, then the teachers will give meaningful knowledge in return, which will lead to a marketable credential, which will then provide access to a rewarding job. While most students are willing to accept

this bargain, the lads are not. They reject the moral authority upon which the formal structure of the school depends, a rejection that rests upon a reasonable calculation of their own chances for success and upon a realistic appraisal of the requirements demanded by the type of work that is likely to be available to them. . . . While the lads' resistance is counterproductive in the long run, it is nevertheless effective for them in the short run. (Emphasis added)

(Feinberg & Soltis, 1992, p. 66)

You must establish legitimacy with your students if they are going to respect both you and what you have to offer them in the classroom. Obtaining legitimacy is like accumulating a form of "currency" with your students. Once you have it, you can then choose how you want to spend it. And just how do you spend this "currency"? You spend it on helping them arrive at good decisions about their education and their behavior in your classroom.

While this may be relatively easy with students who have academic ambitions (you are helping them obtain "an entrance ticket" to their next level of schooling), it is very difficult to do this with kids who do not see a future for themselves that involves further education.

If you fail to show your students that what you are teaching is important *to them*, if you fail to show your students that you care about them and their success in life, and if you fail to make a commitment to them that you will be there for them and work for what is good for them, then you have failed to establish legitimacy.

The result? Some of your students will challenge your authority—just like the lads did—and you will most certainly have classroom discipline issues.

Teachers who have established legitimacy and teachers who have established real authority with their students have no need to throw their weight around or flex their classroom muscle.

Why should your students listen to you? Why should they cooperate with you? Why should they respect you? Those are fair questions—and you should better have some good answers ready when students ask you those questions.

By the way: You can begin the process of establishing legitimacy on the first day of class. On day 1, you should distribute a *letter of introduction* about yourself to your students. In this letter, tell them some personal things about yourself (where you grew up and went to school, how you did in school, some information about your family, different jobs you have had, etc.). Then move into a brief description of your professional life, your education, your teaching experiences, your publications, and the like.

Deliberately reveal some aspects about yourself and your life that they do not expect. Let them see you as a person—not just as a teacher—right from the first day of school.

Depending on the age level of the students, you can then have them write a letter of introduction back to you in which they use your letter to them as a template. This has proven a very effective way for teachers to begin the process of establishing legitimacy, something that is foundational to a teacher's success with any group of students.

Another way to help establish legitimacy and relate the curriculum to the interests of the students is through the information you obtained in the Newspaper of the Self project. Once you discover what your students are interested in, there are myriad creative ways to tie in the curriculum to their interests. For example, students may not care much for a math problem that begins with, "A train left New York heading west at an average speed of X, while a train left Los Angeles heading east at an average speed of Y . . ."

However, if you have a group of students who are into skateboarding, for example, you can easily adapt the question to skateboarding.

Establishing legitimacy is difficult, partially because it is so contextual. How you go about establishing legitimacy will vary from school to school, and from class to class. Teachers do this in many ways, and it is simply not possible to go into great depth here on how to do this without knowing the specifics of a particular classroom.

The important thing for you as a teacher is to recognize that the onus for establishing legitimacy is on *you*, and if you can accomplish this, learning will skyrocket in your classroom.

24. FIRED UP? READY TO GO?

Class starts earlier for the teacher than it does for the students. You cannot walk into the classroom at the same time as the students and expect things to go well.

You need to arrive at your classroom well before the first student walks through the door. You need to have everything in place that you will need for your teaching day, and you yourself must be physically, mentally, and emotionally ready to teach.

This means that you have made sure that the technology is connected to the network. This means that all of your printed copies are ready for distribution and you have enough copies for each student (with a few extras). This means that you have enough books, notebooks or laptops, extra pens, pencils, and paper for the students who have forgotten their supplies.

It also means that you are mentally and physically ready to teach!

During Barack Obama's first run for the presidency in 2008, he used the theme: *Fired up! Ready to go!*

Obama tells the story that he first heard this from a woman in a small hall in South Carolina where he was campaigning. He had arrived at the hall after a long drive. It was pouring rain outside and—being without an umbrella—he

Figure 2.2.

was soaked by the time he got from the car into the hall. The people in the room did not appear all too pleased to see him. The feeling in the hall was lethargic and gloomy.

Then a woman sitting in the back of the room yelled: "Fired up?" And the twenty or so people sitting in the hall yelled back, "Fired up!"

She then yelled, "Ready to go?" And the twenty or so people sitting in the hall yelled back, "Ready to go!"

This woman, with her chant, had inserted energy into the entire audience, and into Obama himself. He felt energized, the audience felt energized, and the entire event was transformed in a most positive way.

That chant became a theme in Obama's campaign. It also became a theme in my teaching.

There are teachers who keep a poster at their desks that ask: "Fired up?" "Ready to go?" They do this because they want to be fired up and ready to go every time they walk into their classrooms because they believe their students deserve no less.

That is how *you* need to start each of your classes, "Fired up!" and "Ready to go!" (*really* ready to go). *Your* students deserve no less.

25. LET HORTON THE ELEPHANT BE YOUR ROLE MODEL

In the famous Dr. Seuss book, *Horton Hatches the Egg*, Horton the Elephant is tricked into promising to sit on a bird's egg, while the mother bird—Lazy Mayzie—takes a very long vacation in Palm Beach.

Horton goes through a number of hardships that tempt him to forgo his promise to sit on the egg.

When those around him attempt to get Horton to abandon the egg, Horton replies: "I meant what I said, and I said what I meant. An elephant's faithful, one hundred percent."

There is a wonderful lesson in this story for teachers.

When talking to your students—mean what you say and say what you mean. Never bluff your students! Never lie to your students! Always—*always*—follow through and do what you said you would do!

This message bears repeating. Never bluff your students! Never lie to your students! Always follow through and do what you said you would do!

The problem with bluffing your students—saying you are going to do something, then not following through—is that they will catch on to this very quickly. They will then begin to question—sometimes overtly, sometimes unconsciously—whether or not you are going to follow through on any of your commitments.

This applies to "good things," such as "If you work hard this class, I will give you more time in the gym," and it also applies to "bad things," such as "If you don't get to work right now I am going to keep the whole class in at recess!"

In either case, *you simply cannot bluff!* If you say these kinds of things and don't follow through, you will very quickly lose the trust and confidence of your students.

This is much like the parent who yells at their child, "If you don't get off that computer right now, I will ground you for a month!" The kid had heard this many times before, and the longest she/he has ever been grounded from the computer for was a day. In examples such as this, the threat is empty because the promised outcome is never carried through.

A caution here.

Because you will want to have your students know that you *always* follow through on what you say, *you need to be very careful what you say.* You simply cannot say things in anger that you are then unable to follow through on. *You must be very careful with your words.*

Remember, be like Horton, mean what you say and say what you mean.

26. EVEN MONKEYS KNOW WHEN SOMETHING IS UNFAIR

In a TED Talk published on April 4, 2013, Frans de Waal showed an experiment he conducted with two Capuchin monkeys.

The monkeys were placed in two Plexiglas cages side by side. A researcher would give the monkeys food if the monkeys passed the researcher a pebble that had been placed in the cages.

When the researcher gave each monkey a piece of cucumber, each of the monkeys was satisfied and would consistently pass the researcher a pebble in order to obtain a piece of cucumber.

However, the researcher then made a small but significant change. She gave the first monkey a piece of cucumber in exchange for a pebble, and the first monkey quite happily ate the cucumber. Then she gave the second monkey a *grape* in exchange for a pebble. The first monkey saw this.

The first monkey was then cued to give a pebble, which it did. When the researcher then gave this monkey a piece of cucumber, it threw the cucumber at the researcher and began screaming and shaking its cage. Cucumber was no longer good enough—it wanted a grape, just like the second monkey had received. Capuchin monkeys can see right away when something is unfair.

If Capuchin monkeys can catch on to unfairness so fast, imagine how quickly your students will catch on to unfairness in the classroom from you.

Figure 2.3.

Kids have an acute sense of what is fair and what is not. If students in your class see you as being unfair, of showing favoritism, you will be in for a very rough ride.

Being fair sounds easy to do, but in actuality it can be quite challenging.

For example, teachers tend to like students who are like them. If you are athletic and play a lot of sports, you might find yourself talking to the kids in your class who play sports more than those who don't. This can be especially true at playoff time. When the Stanley Cup finals or the NBA finals are on—and you as a teacher are very invested in your favorite teams and how they are doing—it is hard not to talk about this with the kids in your class who are really interested in these events as well.

Gender can also be at play here.

A few years ago a group of high school girls approached their favorite teacher to complain that "Miss X favored the boys" and they were very resentful of this. Whether this perceived favoritism was true is not the point; it was certainly true in the eyes of these young ladies, and because of this perception, the teacher who "favored the boys" had a great deal of trouble with the girls in her class.

Punishing the whole class for the transgressions of a few kids is another blatantly unfair—though not uncommon—way that teachers treat students unfairly. Kids have an acute sense of fairness, and this kind of discipline is grossly unfair and students know it.

Treat kids fairly. Do not show favoritism. While it is easy to like and favor kids who are nice and who work hard and who don't smell badly, that is a trap.

All of the students will see this—the ones you favor and the ones you don't—and this will certainly cause difficulties for you.

By the way: When you ask a question of the entire class, then pick one student to respond—often, that student will not be very happy with you. In their mind, they may be thinking, "Why did she/he pick on me? What did I do?" This is especially true if the student didn't raise his or her hand.

Here is an excellent strategy for asking students questions or placing them into working groups in a way that the kids will see as being very fair.

On the first day of school (or very early in the first week) pass out one playing card to each student, and have them print their name on the card (or you may choose to do this yourself before the school year starts). Collect the cards. You now have a set of playing cards with each student's name on them.

Now, when you ask a question of the entire class, tell your students, "No hands! All of you are responsible for thinking of an answer to this question." Give them time to think of their answer (remember "wait time"), then draw a card out of the deck, and ask that person to respond. Or you may choose to have your students draw cards from the deck.

In this way, *all* students are held accountable for being prepared to answer the questions you ask, and *none* of them can blame you for choosing them and think you are being unfair—it is simply the luck of the draw.

The playing cards also work well if you want to put your students into random groups for a particular activity. Let's say you want to put your class into five random groups. Simply deal these cards face down into five piles and you have your groups. Again, the students can't be upset with you or consider the groupings as unfair as it is all totally random—again, simply the luck of the draw.

27. WHEN YOU ARE VASTLY OUTNUMBERED, FIGHTING IS UNWISE

In the ancient Chinese book, *The Art of War*—written approximately 2,500 years ago—Sun Tzu (2011) advises that the first step necessary for victory is to *know when to fight and when not to fight.* That was good advice then, and it is good advice now.

And yet, some teachers *still* choose to fight with their students, and they choose to do so on a consistent basis throughout the school year. This is a foolish and ultimately unwinnable strategy. Why?

First, the obvious—your students have you outnumbered. There are often twenty-five to thirty students and only one teacher. The odds are never in your favor.

Second, as a group, they have more energy than you do as an individual. They can and they will wear you down if you choose to do battle with them on an ongoing basis. The truth of this gets even more evident as you deal with kids as they get older throughout the grades.

Circumstances may arise, however, when you have no choice but to deal with a conflict involving a student or group of students. When that happens, be sure to figure out some way that you can win. What does winning mean in these types of situations? It means that you have figured out a way to effectively *deal with the actual problem, and still maintain an effective working relationship with the student(s)* after the problem has been dealt with.

Even when you walk into a classroom at the beginning of the year where some students automatically view you as the teacher and therefore as being "the enemy," don't fall into the trap that they will surely lay as they begin fighting with you. As Max Lucado says, "Conflict is inevitable. Combat is optional." This has remarkable relevance to classroom teaching—especially in regard to students as they get older.

You simply cannot win a war with your students.

The only way to truly "win" is to "win them over." And how do you "win them over"?

It begins on the very first day (remember #18: you never get a second chance to make a first impression). When you first meet your students, show them some aspect of who you are *as a person*—not just as a teacher. Kids can sometimes view you as only your role. Let them into your life outside of school a little bit—albeit in an appropriate way.

Over the next few weeks at the beginning of the school year, show that you genuinely care about them and their success as students and as persons. And remember this important fact: *you cannot fake sincerity—your kids will know if you really care about them or not.*

Additionally, you must prepare and deliver lessons that are engaging, relevant, fun, and at the appropriate level of challenge in your classroom. Your classroom needs to be a place where work and play start to blur and blend together.

Be sure that you treat them fairly—both as a group and as individuals. That is an essential component of a healthy and effective student-teacher working relationship. You simply cannot be successful without it.

If you are able to do these things on a consistent basis, there will be very little conflict in your classroom, and a great deal of learning.

28. THE IMPORTANCE OF FACE

Anyone who has spent time with children knows that as they get older, the opinions of their friends and peers begin to mean more and more to them. This typically begins to develop in upper elementary school, is in full bloom by junior/high-middle school, and generally continues on throughout high school. How their classmates view them matters a great deal to most students.

Game theory talks about "payoffs"—the reward that a player gets for "winning." Let's look at some of the various kinds of student payoffs in terms of behavior and how students sometimes choose to gain or lose face with their peers.

If you chose to discipline or embarrass a student in front of others, the student will likely feel that he or she is "losing face." They will probably feel ashamed and resentful, and they will need to respond to you in some way.

Some students in this situation may stay silent and feel embarrassed—and will likely resent you for what you have done to them for a very long time. Others will stay silent at the time and will get even with you in some way later on.

Still others—those with strength or who feel they have a lot to lose by taking what you are dishing out—these students will attack you in front of the class. The "payoff" for them is that they feel they are saving face and keeping (or gaining) the respect of their peers.

If this happens, you are now in a situation where you are attempting to correct a student, the student isn't accepting this, and there are twenty-plus kids watching the performance, wondering who is going to "win."

All of this is avoidable.

First, it is incumbent upon you to *deescalate* situations like this. If the student yells at you, and you yell back even louder, your behavior is adding more tension to this situation. If the student yells, you need to remain calm and talk softly. Your task is to *decrease the tension*, not add to it through an inappropriate response. Put another way, you need to become a *calming down expert*.

Second, you almost always want to correct behavior by dealing with the student *in isolation*. (See #29 for how to accomplish this.)

In a corrective discipline situation, almost all students will behave very differently in front of the class than if you are interacting with them alone. When you are interacting with them alone, what you are getting is the student *himself/herself*—the private, authentic student—not the "public student" who needs to impress his or her friends.

When you are dealing with students in front of their peers, what you are getting is the public face they feel they have to display—and in these circumstances, it is very difficult to get to the root of the conflict and find a way forward that is going to work for both you and the student.

Alone with the student is better.

As well, it is most important that you remember this: the next day, both you and the student will be back in the classroom—and every other school day for the remainder of the year. You need to determine how to deal with a student's inappropriate behavior in ways that do not permanently damage your working relationship with that student.

Why? Because realistically, the two of you are going to spend a lot of time together over the course of the school year, so it is in both of your best interests that you figure out a solution to a conflict situation that works for both of you.

29. NEVER LOOK BACK WHEN ASKING A STUDENT TO FOLLOW YOU OUT OF THE CLASSROOM

In #28, we discussed how important it is when in conflict situations with a student by getting the student away from the audience of their peers and talking to them alone.

This of course raises the question, how do you get students alone and out of the classroom?

This can be difficult if the situation in the classroom has already begun to heat up and you are unsure if the student will leave the classroom and step out into the hall as you want them to.

Here is a strategy that rarely fails. When you ask a student to step out of the classroom and into the hallway for a private conversation (and you will want to ask them to do this quietly and discreetly)—exit the classroom immediately after making your request, and *without looking back*.

Never look back!

If you look back to see *if* the student is following you into the hallway, this implies that you are *unsure* if she/he is coming. This gives the impression to the student (albeit probably at an unconscious level) that she/he has a choice, and the student will very likely pick up on this unintended cue.

It is far better for you to simply walk out of the classroom and directly into the hallway. Move away from the door so the student cannot see you, and wait in the hallway.

Do not look back into the classroom. Just wait.

It has been the experience of most teachers that the student will virtually *always* follow you out of the room, and she/he will do so fairly quickly.

Once you get them alone, out of the classroom, you can then have a quiet and productive conversation about what you are going to agree to do to address the problem that got the student into the hallway in the first place.

The conversation, the understanding, and the negotiation have begun.

By the way: When you go about having this private conversation with a student in the hallway, this is *not* your opportunity to berate the student. Most often, what you will want to do is to give the student the chance to be heard, to explain why the student is behaving the way he or she is. This involves asking probing questions in a quiet, calm voice and then listening carefully to the answers. It involves *holding the student accountable for his or her behavior and choices* and having the student come up with a plan to change the behavior to reenter your classroom. It is important that you insist that the student explain his or her behavior and why he or she chose to be inappropriate. It is also important that you insist the student to come up with a plan to change his or her behavior before he or she can reenter your classroom.

Be careful here. When you ask students, "What will you do to change your behavior in order to get back into class?" many students will shrug their shoulders and respond, "I don't know." This is a trap. Do *not* come up with a plan for them. Rather, respond with something like, "If I leave you in the hallway to come up with a *written plan* to change your behavior, how long do you think it will take you?" Most students would rather talk than write—and therefore most students will then quickly come up with a plan to get back into class.

As well, it is important to remember that in situations such as this, you will do most of the listening.

30. DON'T JUST STAND THERE—*DO SOMETHING!*

During a workshop entitled "Student Discipline" given by a child psychologist a few years ago, the presenter described one discipline technique which he called "extinguishing." He encouraged us teachers to "extinguish" inappropriate behavior in our students by simply ignoring it. He argued that if students didn't get any attention from a particular behavior, then they would stop the behavior.

This advice is analogous to saying, "Ignore the fire in the classroom. If you wait long enough, it will eventually stop burning." True—it will stop burning eventually—after the school had burned down!

If you choose to ignore unacceptable behaviors in your students, when it is clear to your students that you have seen and/or have heard it, your students will reach one of two conclusions.

if you are relying on technology or a guest speaker as key components of your lesson.

Most teachers like technology and all the advantages it brings to their classrooms. Having said that, prudent teachers always have a "felt marker and white board" or "paper and pencil" backup lesson plan ready for when the technology goes down or the guest speaker doesn't show up.

There's a reason that paper and pencil have been around for centuries— very high reliability, very low complexity. We cannot say the same thing about laptops or smartboards.

Remember this the next time you are planning a lesson that is entirely technology based—have a Plan B.

34. WHAT DID YOU LEARN IN SCHOOL TODAY?

There will likely be times after school or during supper when the parents/ caregivers of your students look at them and ask, "What did you learn at school today?"

A question for you to consider is this: How will *your* students respond when they are asked this question?

All too often, kids respond to this question with a shrug of the shoulders and reply, "Nothing."

You need to remember that *your best ambassadors to the parents/caregivers of your students are your students themselves*. It is they who will bring home the stories of what happened at school that day. It is they who will respond to the question, "What did you learn at school today?" if asked that question at home in the evening.

The parents/caregivers of your students will start to form impressions of you based on the stories their kids bring home about you and based on their children's responses to questions such as "What did you learn at school today?"

Therefore, you will want to ensure that when *your students* go home and are asked, "What did you learn at school today?" they do *not* reply, *"Nothing!"*

How do you do this? You do this through your *classroom exit strategy*. Let's explore what this can look like.

Early in the first week of school, you will want to tell your students that it is important for you that their parents/caregivers know that you—as their child's teacher—are capable and that you are working hard each day to teach their children. After all, their tax dollars are paying your salary, so you owe it to them and your students to do your job and to do it well.

You would then go over the scenario of how bad it makes you look to the parents/caregivers of your students if they go home and are asked, "What did you learn at school today?" and they reply, "Nothing." That response makes you—their teacher—look lazy, or incompetent, or both. And since you certainly do not want to look lazy and/or incompetent, you need your students to develop a better answer. "Nothing" is not an acceptable answer, nor is it honest, because your students *had* learned some things in school that day, just as they will every day of this school year.

So, you need to develop a number of classroom *exit strategies* so your students remember what it is they learned each day.

Near the end of a class in secondary schools (where teachers often teach a number of different classes each day) or at the end of the day in elementary schools (where teachers often teach the same class for most—if not all—of the day), tell your students that today you will stand at the classroom door, and as they try to exit the classroom, you will ask them this question, "If your parent/caregiver asks you what did you learn at school today, how will you reply?" If they give you an acceptable answer, you can respond with, "Have a nice evening" and let them go. If their answer is unacceptable, they must go to the end of the line of kids trying to leave the room and have a better answer ready by the time they get back to you.

Another type of exit strategy is to distribute index cards or Post-it notes to your students just prior to the end of classes and have them write down their response to the question, "If your parent/caregiver asks you what did you learn at school today—how will you reply?" Students are then required to hand you their written response at the classroom door as their "exit ticket" and you can glance at their response and let them go on their way if their response is acceptable. This method takes less time than the verbal responses in the previous example.

For older students, you may choose to have them write a "daily reflection"—a paragraph of no more than three to five sentences in which they describe the most important or interesting thing they learned that day and why this particular learning stood out for them.

This is not something that ought to be done at the end of every day or every class, but it is something that you want to do it often early in the school year, then more randomly throughout the remainder of the year. Remember, *you never get a second chance to make a first impression*, and you want the parents/caregivers of your students to have a very good first impression of you and what you are teaching their children early in the school year. This strategy is one way to help you achieve this.

By the way: There is another additional benefit to you as a teacher if you do the exit strategy with your students. Teachers are often quite surprised by their students' responses to the question, "What did you learn at school today?" Teachers know what they have taught, but they don't know what students have learned unless they check.

There are many times when a teacher will read an exit Post-it note or listen to one of their students reply to the question, "If your parent/caregiver asks you what did you learn at school today—how will you reply?" and they will be surprised by the student's response. Students may enlighten their teachers on some learning they had that day that for the teacher was relatively insignificant, but for the student was really important.

Students' answers to this question can give you a great deal of insight into *what they have learned*, not just *what you have taught*. And at times, you will discover that there is quite a difference.

Section Three

What You Need to Do during the First Month

INTRODUCTION

At this point, you have made it to the end of your first week of teaching. Congratulations!

Please understand that all of the work that you did in the first week to establish classroom procedures and set behavioral expectations and begin to develop effective student-teacher relationships with your students is not over. In fact, it is never really over until the school year is over. These are things that constantly need revisiting throughout the school year to tweak, improve, or revise. You are not done working on these things just because the first week is over. Please keep that in mind.

Nonetheless, you can now start thinking about some of the bigger picture aspects of your teaching practices and of yourself as a teacher.

This section will give you some ideas in regard to what you will face during that first month of teaching and some strategies as to how to successfully deal with these.

35. EYES OPEN; EARS OPEN; MOUTH CLOSED

Very few, if any, of the teachers at your school who have been teaching there for several years will think that you—if you are a beginning teacher or if you are new to the school—have much to say just quite yet about how things ought to be run in classrooms and at the school as a whole.

For the first month (or second, or third, or. . .) that you are a new teacher at *any* school, you would be well advised to keep your *eyes open*, keep your *ears open*, and your *mouth shut* about your thoughts, feelings, and perceptions of the school, especially around your colleagues.

Figure 3.1.

This is particularly important to do at staff meetings.

The exception to the "mouth shut rule" is when you are asking questions of colleagues or mentors to gain information as to how to be a better teacher and/or how things work at your new school.

Spend the first few months at any new school (even if you are an experienced teacher who has moved to a new school) learning in depth and detail how and why your school runs the way it does before criticizing things or advocating for changes.

In order to learn about your students, in order to learn about your colleagues, in order to learn about the school community, you will need to *pay attention*. You will need to *be mindful*; you will need to *be present*; you will need to *be aware*. These are not easy to do. There are so many distractions, and our minds tend to wander at the best of times. However, when you are no longer truly present to what is going on in your classroom or your school, you have stopped learning.

Put simply, you cannot learn from experience unless you are fully present to the experience.

By the way: In his book *Make Your Bed,* William McRaven (2017), a retired U.S. Navy Admiral, describes his training as a Navy SEAL recruit. One of the lessons the instructors stressed was this: *You can't go it alone.* SEAL recruits were required to carry a large raft with them wherever they went—a task they could only accomplish as a group. McRaven learned early that it takes a team of people to accomplish a mission; one person simply cannot do it alone.

As a teacher, you too will most certainly need the help of others if you want to become or to remain a good teacher.

First, you will need a mentor or two (and this is particularly true if you are a beginning teacher). So when you arrive at your first school (or any new school after that), watch carefully. Whom do other teachers go to for advice? Who is the teacher who gets the respect of colleagues when he or she speaks at meetings or in the staff room? This person has a lot to offer you. Approach him or her and work to establish a mentor-protégé relationship with him or her. This person has a great deal to teach you, and you would be well served if he or she agrees to take on the role as your mentor.

As well, if you are lucky enough to have a mentor teacher who teaches the same courses as you do and who is willing to share the teaching and assessment materials with you, let him or her know how grateful you are. These teachers have likely spent hundreds of hours developing these materials, and you are the lucky beneficiary of all of this work. It is not something they have to do, and it is a gift that will save you hundreds of hours of preparation time. Such a gift should be appropriately acknowledged.

Remember the lesson from the Navy SEALs: *You can't go it alone.*

36. THE BEST TEACHERS YOU WILL EVER HAVE

If you want to really learn the best ways to teach a particular group of students, the only ones who can teach you how to do that to any great depth are . . . that particular group of students.

Great teaching requires first that you be truly present to your students, that you pay attention. Pay attention to what? Pay attention to what your students are trying to teach *you* about teaching *them*. Pay very close attention. They will tell you, and they will show you, what works with them and for them—as well as what does not.

As was mentioned earlier, you cannot learn from experience unless you first take notice of the experience. In his book *A Life in Parts*, Bryan Cranston (2016) of *Breaking Bad* fame says, "The best teacher is experience. Find the educational in every situation." Good advice, but you have to be attentive to your experiences in order to do this.

Every day you teach, you will be presented with the opportunity for learning experiences. Note that this is an *opportunity*—not a *guarantee*. You will learn from these experiences only if you are attentive and open to learning from them.

These experiences will present opportunities for you to grow as a teacher. Unfortunately, teachers can—and often do—disregard these experiences, learning little or nothing from them. Our habits and our laziness can lure us away from authentic learning about how to teach our students—the students we have with us *this year*—the ones that are different from the students we had *last year*.

It takes energy, focus, and attentiveness to be truly present to what is happening in our classrooms now and to learn from this.

Some teachers keep a journal in which, at the end of the day, they simply make a short note about one major thing they learned about teaching and/or their students that day.

Some examples are things like: "Billy loves dogs and has a puppy." "Susie's dad is really ill." "I need to give each person specific roles for them to do before we do group work again." "My instructions were too vague; I need to break them down into smaller steps and write them on the whiteboard." "I spend too much time at the front of the room and the kids at the back are being neglected." "I need to start asking higher-level questions more often."

If you choose to do this, by the end of the school year, you have almost 200 learnings. Not a bad year.

37. SECRETARIES, CUSTODIANS, AND TEACHER AIDES

Some teachers tend to think that because they have a university degree and are "professional staff" that makes them in some way superior to the "non-professional staff." That is a big mistake.

It is a wise teacher who is kind and respectful to the school's support staff, especially the secretaries, custodians, and teacher aides. They all play exceptionally important roles in making a school function well.

Throughout the school year, there will come numerous times when you will need the help of your school's support staff (and please remember, they likely don't need you very much). You will need them to help make your classroom cleaner, you will need them to assist you with disruptive kids, you will need them to do emergency copying for you, and so on.

With their help, you will be a more effective teacher—and in the end, this will benefit your students.

Treat school support staff well and honor the work they do. Their work matters and makes the school as a whole run better.

Remember: if you are looking down on people, it is highly unlikely that they will be looking up to you. And it is a certainty that if you treat your school's support staff badly, they will not go out of their way to help you and the students you teach.

38. WHO KNEW? TEN MINUTES IS A HUGE CHUNK OF TIME

Most teachers lament that there is never enough time to do everything they need to accomplish in order to be a successful teacher. The complaint that "there is not enough time!" is one of the most prevalent grumbles heard from the majority of teachers in the majority of schools all over this planet.

Time is the one resource in teaching that once spent you cannot get back.

In order to combat this, if you want to be a successful teacher, you must learn to *manage your minutes*.

Some teachers think they need huge chunks of time to accomplish big things. However, successful teachers have made the amazing discovery that *ten minutes is a huge chunk of time*. They have discovered that they can accomplish a great deal of work in just ten minutes, and that if they add just another ten minutes to the first ten minutes, they can accomplish even more.

When it comes to having your students achieve the learning goals that you have set out for them during any given lesson, do *not* think in terms of days, hours, class periods, or blocks. Think in terms of *minutes*, and spend every minute carefully and in ways that move you toward your teaching goals. In other words, *manage your minutes!*

In schools, this is also referred to as *time on task*—which examines how much time in classrooms is actually being spent on curriculum and learning as compared to other classroom activities. While all teachers must deal with events in their classrooms such as taking attendance, collecting field trip forms, listening to announcements, going to school assemblies, and the like, good teachers work hard to keep these activities to a minimum because they all take away from precious instructional time.

And the amount of time lost to noninstructional activities in schools can be staggering. In an article published in *Educational Leadership* (May 1984), Nancy Karweit tells us that in many schools, "only about half the time in the school day is used for instruction." Think about that for a moment.

If you want your students to learn, you will have to work very diligently on maximizing the time you have with them to ensure that the majority of that time is spent engaged in learning activities.

Please remember this quote from Todd Whitaker: "The best part of teaching is that it matters. The hardest part of teaching is that every moment matters every day."

39. MAYBE NOT FIFTY SHADES OF GRAY—BUT FORTY-NINE FOR SURE

In his book *Sapiens: A Brief History of Humankind*, Yuval Harari (2016) argues that in education today, there is a strong movement toward the *exact sciences*—which he defines as *exact* due to their use of mathematical tools. Even in education—where we study the humanities via disciplines such as psychology, sociology, political science, and philosophy—there is a strong push toward the use of statistics as a tool that can be used to make these disciplines more precise.

You are a teacher, and you need to understand this one immutable fact: *teaching is not an exact science!*

You are working primarily with children and young adults—not numbers. As much as a student or a group of students can be stable and steady, they can in equal measure be unpredictable, emotional, erratic, inconsistent, and variable.

They can be pleasant, attentive, and eager to learn one day, and angry, disinterested, and withdrawn the next. And on any given school day, any student may be at either end of this continuum, or at any of the many stops in between. You may even see them move back and forth along this continuum several times during a single class.

If you are a person who prefers predictability and stability, you are not going to find it in a classroom. Looking for predictability and repetitiveness in student behavior in a classroom is like looking for a carton of milk in a hardware store—you're simply not going to find it there.

If, however, you are a person who loves variety, adventure, the challenge of the unknown, and the unpredictable on a day-to-day basis, the classroom will be a great fit for you.

You need to learn to *accept your students for who they are on any given school day.*

And don't worry too much if a particular student is having a bad day. Students are much like the weather—just be patient and wait—they will change.

40. WHAT'S THE DIFFERENCE BETWEEN A CLASSROOM AND A PETRI DISH?

When you graduate from university or leave a secondary school teaching position to teach in an elementary school, you may find that you are ill a lot more often than in previous years. You may find yourself coming down with colds or the flu much more frequently. Why is this? What is going?

Schools are *very* germy places. They are filled with kids who come from homes filled with other people, all of whom can play host to germs, viruses, and the like. Thus, the school and the classroom are often home to billions of bacteria and viruses.

But elementary school brings with it a whole new level of contamination. If you teach elementary school and are outside walking around on supervision, it is only a matter of minutes before some little kid will run up behind you and grab your hand to walk with you.

A sweet, friendly gesture to be sure. However, God only knows where that hand has been or the last time it was thoroughly washed.

Figure 3.2.

And to make this situation worse, little children touch everything with their oft-germy little hands. Virtually everything you touch in school is a cesspool of bacteria and viruses.

What can you do to help prevent yourself from becoming sick in an environment as germ-filled as your school? You must

1. wash your hands constantly;
2. have hand sanitizer at your desk;
3. think very seriously about getting the flu shot every fall;
4. have two boxes of tissue in your classroom, one for you and one for your students; and
5. use your own pens, pencils, staplers, and so on. To be sure, you want these kinds of supplies available for your students to use, but smart teachers keep their supplies separate from the student supplies. Do this, and your sinuses will thank you.

If you don't take these steps, you will have more colds and flus than you have ever had in your life—especially if you teach elementary students.

Why is this less likely to occur in junior high-middle schools or in high schools? Because as your students get older, the social space between students and teachers becomes greater, and also because as most students get older, they become more aware of the proper habits of personal hygiene.

To answer the original question: What's the difference between a classroom and a petri dish? Answer: *Nothing* . . . as far as bacteria and viruses are concerned. Both are terrific places to breed.

41. WANT TO AVOID CLASSROOM CHAOS? BAIT THE HOOK TO SUIT THE FISH!

Many teachers think that effective classroom discipline has to do with how a teacher deals with students *after* they have misbehaved in some way.

Some teachers also tend to think of discipline as a particular *set of techniques* that work along the lines of: "*If* the student does this kind of bad behavior, *then* the teacher responds this way. *If* the student makes that kind of inappropriate choice, *then* the teacher responds that way."

It's as if student discipline is a series of "if–then" steps. This thinking is fundamentally incorrect.

Good student discipline finds its genesis in excellent classroom management. Good student discipline is at its heart *preventative*—you prevent discipline issues from happening in the first place. This is not a new idea. Over 2,000 years ago, Lao-tzu (who has been described as one of the greatest teachers in history) advised in *Tao Te Ching* that we would be well advised to "prevent trouble before it arises." This is at the very heart of effective classroom management. He also advises that we should "put things in order before they exist" (Mitchell, 1988). Think here about how effective teachers have their classrooms arranged *prior* to school even beginning and how well prepared they are to teach well *before* the lessons actually take place.

The best way to prevent poor student behavior is first of all by having well-prepared and engaging lessons that are relevant to the lives of your students, that you are excited to teach, and that are delivered in a physical environment that is structured to support student learning.

That statement is easy to write, easy to understand, and incredibly difficult to do. But the payoff in terms of student learning and minimizing student discipline issues is absolutely amazing.

Students who are *engaged with learning content that is interesting and relevant to them* are far too busy working with the content, one another, and the teacher to get into much trouble.

Dale Carnegie once said: "Personally I am very fond of strawberries and cream, but I have found that for some strange reason, fish prefer worms. So when I went fishing, I didn't think about what *I wanted*. I thought about what *they wanted*. I didn't bait the hook with strawberries and cream. Rather, I dangled a worm or grasshopper in front of the fish."

Good teachers do this. Good teachers "bait the hook to suit the fish."

Ask these questions about your students: What do *they* want? What makes *them* tick? What are *they* interested in? Then figure out ways to make your lessons interesting and relevant to your students.

Good teachers know that if a class is to be successful in terms of student learning, then it *must work for the students* as well as for the teacher. Any class that works only for the teacher, but not for the students, doesn't really work at all.

In the movie *Dead Poets Society*, John Keating (a teacher played by Robin Williams) is given a job in 1959 to teach poetry at an elite all-boys prep school in Vermont. His students are all in their mid-teens—not a time in life when young men are particularly interested in poetry. But what are boys generally interested in at that age?

Mr. Keating asks the boys in his poetry class a question: "Language was developed for one endeavor, and that is?" One of the boys responds, "To communicate."

Mr. Keating replies, "No . . . to woo women!"

Now this was something these teenage boys were interested in, and Mr. Keating knew it. He had "baited the hook to suit the fish."

Great lessons delivered with enthusiasm, excitement, and *relevance* will prevent well over 90 percent of discipline problems from ever happening in the first place.

So remember when you are preparing lessons: *Bait the hook to suit the fish!*

By the way: We have already discussed the other single most powerful tool in your "teaching tools box" that has a major impact on minimizing student discipline issues. In #20, we explored the importance—beginning on the very first day of school—of establishing *effective classroom procedures and routines.*

Successful teachers are teachers who (1) have established effective classroom routines; and (2) deliver relevant, interesting, and engaging lessons with passion and enthusiasm to their students.

These teachers *rarely* have student discipline issues. That is their secret! Now, you know it too.

42. HOW TO TRAIN A TIGER: THE ART OF NEGOTIATING WITH YOUR STUDENTS

Sometime ago, there was a documentary on TV about a man who trained animals for movies. This individual was quite famous for the effectiveness of his work, and the documentary showed the techniques he used to train birds, dogs, cats, and finally it showed him working with a very large tiger.

This particular tiger still had both its claws and its teeth—very large claws; very large teeth.

The interviewer asked the animal trainer, "What do you do when the tiger doesn't obey you—when the tiger doesn't do what you want her to do?"

The trainer smiled and replied, "Well, sometimes I get what I want, and sometimes the tiger gets what she wants." (Ripley, 2016, p. 4)

Life in a classroom is a bit like that—sometimes the teacher gets what they want; sometimes the students get what they want. This is especially true as students get older, more aware, and develop ideas and opinions of their own. Any teacher who thinks students ought to "do what they're told because I'm the teacher" is in for a very quick wake-up call. While this can be more of an issue in junior high-middle school or high school, students in elementary grades can challenge a teacher's authority as well.

A teacher colleague of mine named Bob told me a story about a student teacher he worked with while he was teaching elementary music. The student teacher was in his mid-thirties. He was hardworking and very knowledgeable in regard to music.

After a couple of weeks of observing Bob teach, the student teacher began teaching some of the classes on his own, with Bob observing the class.

One day, while the student teacher was instructing a Grade 4 music class, Bob asked the student teacher if it would be OK if he left the room for a couple of minutes to grab a coffee from the staff room.

Figure 3.3

"Not a problem," the student teacher replied. "I've got this under control; no worries."

Bob left the music room, grabbed his coffee, and walked back to the music room. He had been gone for less than three minutes.

As Bob turned the corner and entered the hallway leading to the music room on his way back to the class, he saw the student teacher in the hallway with one of the Grade 4 boys from the class.

The student teacher was down on his knees; he had both his hands on the boy's shirt at the front of the collar; and he had the kid pinned to the wall. The boy's feet were off the ground.

"Who's the boss?" Bob heard the student teacher yell at the boy.

Through his choked throat, the boy squeaked back in reply, "I am!"

"Who's the boss?" Clearly, this student teacher saw a power structure in the classroom with him at the top. His young student had a different point of view.

In classrooms that work really well, the answer to the question "Who's the boss?" is most often, "Well, it depends."

There is a great deal of negotiation that goes on in effective classrooms—sometimes with the class as a whole; often on a student-by-student basis.

Great teachers are a bit like the animal trainer working with the tiger—they understand that in classrooms today, sometimes the teachers get what they want, and sometimes the students get what they want.

Classrooms are about *we*—not *me*. You and your students are in this *together*—and the classroom has to work for *both* of you.

You need to learn *how* to negotiate effectively with your students, as well as *when* to negotiate with your students. It is important to remember that some things in the classroom are *absolutely nonnegotiable*. The procedures and routines that you established in the first week of school are nonnegotiable. The classroom rule regarding not interfering with teaching and learning in the classroom is a nonnegotiable. These are "Ten Commandments" of any good classroom—those behavioral expectations that are "written in stone" and are necessary for the successful functioning of the classroom for all the students and the teacher.

As for the rest of "how we do things in our classroom," good teachers negotiate these with their students and find ways that work for both the students and themselves.

By the way: Perhaps we should take a step back in some circumstances and *celebrate a little rebellion from our students*. It is, after all, one of the characteristics of invention, leadership, and creative thought. Consider the following:

- Pablo Picasso often skipped classes, finding the formality and structure of school unattractive.
- George Bernard Shaw hated schools (he wrote that they were "prisons"), but he went on to win a Nobel Prize in Literature as well as an Oscar.
- Albert Einstein was kicked out of several schools when he was growing up because of his bad attitude and laziness.

Something to think about when the "rebels" in your classrooms don't want to conform.

43. PRACTICE SAYING, "I'M SORRY," AND REALLY MEAN IT

All teachers make mistakes. We make them in the information we tell our students; we make them in the directions we give; we make them in the way we treat our students on certain occasions.

Hopefully, as you gain more experience working with students and as you gather more knowledge about the subjects you teach, you will make fewer and fewer mistakes with each passing year.

However, this still leaves us with the question, "What should you do as a teacher when you do make a mistake?"

The answer is really quite simple. *Apologize sincerely and correct your error.*

There are essentially two types of mistakes you as a teacher can make in a classroom: (1) a mistake with course content or assessment; and (2) a mistake in how you treat your students.

In the case of a mistake in course work (such as an error in the information you provided or an error in assessment), simply apologize and correct the error. These types of mistakes are relatively easy to correct and have no significant long-term consequences that damage your relationship with your students.

However, in the case of mistakes in how a teacher has treated a student, if these are not dealt with quickly and effectively, they can result in permanent damage to an effective student-teacher relationship.

For example, in the case of the student teacher and the Grade 4 boy from the music class, clearly the student teacher's behaviors are unprofessional and unacceptable. He most certainly owes this student a very sincere apology and would be well advised to contact the parents and apologize to them as well. There is nothing that can justify the kind of behavior he did to that child in that circumstance.

In a situation where a teacher mistreats a student in front of his or her class-mates, the teacher then needs to apologize to that student *in front of the class as well.*

If you "lose it" on a kid, you yell and belittle this student in the classroom—with the rest of the class watching—you have done some very serious damage to your relationship with that student. That student has been embarrassed and has lost face in front of his or her peers.

In such a case, *you* need to apologize to that student, *in front of the entire class.* You need to do this sincerely, and after having told the student you have offended what you are going to do and why.

These apologies need to be without excuses. "I was having a bad day" or "Well, Johnny didn't deserve what I did *but* he really is lazy"—these types of apologies are neither helpful nor healing. *No excuses!*

A good apology looks something like, "I'm sorry. My actions were unkind and inappropriate. That will not happen again. I hope you can forgive me."

There is nothing terribly wrong with making mistakes as a teacher. You will make hundreds of them. What would be wrong is if you failed to learn and grow from them. What would be wrong is if you did not try to correct them. And, if you are still making the same mistakes in your fifth year of teaching that you were making in your first year of teaching, well that's just plain dumb.

Be creative! Make new mistakes—and through them, learn something new and become even better.

By the way: Have you ever heard a beginning teacher say, "I want to be mediocre at this job?" Did you say this at the start of your career? Not likely. The vast majority of teachers start their careers wanting to be good teachers.

However, if you think that *being good* equals *being perfect*, you have put yourself in an impossible situation. Some teachers believe that it is their responsibility in regard to their students to "save them all" (we will look at this in more detail in #55). But it is *not* your responsibility to save them all. Not all of them need "saving," and you simply cannot save all of the ones who may need "saving."

If you expect *perfection* of yourself as a teacher, you will always come up short; you will always be disappointed with yourself because there is little in teaching that can be "perfect" (however one defines this).

So please do not expect perfection of yourself as a teacher. This is not good mental health, and if you insist on doing this to yourself, you are a prime candidate for teacher burnout.

Always remember: you should be seeking *progress, not perfection*.

44. GETTING THE ELEPHANT TO GO WHERE YOU WANT IT TO GO

What do you do when a student or a group of students get stubborn and defiant and refuse to do what you want them to do? Some teachers yell. Some teachers threaten. Some teachers send them to the office. None of these strategies is particularly effective.

If you yell a lot, then fairly quickly your students will get used to this, and they will likely tune you out. You yelling at them is likely to be viewed by your students as simply "you being you"—you're the teacher who yells a lot. They quickly stop caring if you're yelling because they've heard you do it so many times before it just doesn't mean much to them anymore.

Likewise, if you threaten your students often but don't follow through, then you will have lost credibility—and the next time you utter a threat, they won't believe you will act on it. Thus, their behavior doesn't change.

If you send students to the office frequently, you are implicitly telling your students that you can't handle them without "mommy or daddy principal" stepping in to help you. Every time you do this, you are weakening your own authority. This also has the downside of displeasing your principal—who is probably busy with other things and may resent doing your classroom discipline for you.

What should you do then?

Think payoff. Kids are generally rationale beings at some level. If they are behaving in a certain way and won't stop that behavior, they are obviously getting something out of the behavior—*their payoff.* Their payoff might be respect from important peers achieved by defying you; it might be getting a few laughs from the class; it might be getting out of doing undesirable school work. Whatever it is, you need to figure out what it is they are getting from their "poor behaviors," because if you don't, you have little chance of taking the best course of action to change those behaviors.

If you are going to *change the behavior*, you need to *change the payoff.*

If the payoff they are getting is from the "audience" (their classmates), then you need to remove the student and isolate them away from this audience.

If the payoff they are getting is that they don't have to do the work ("This is too hard," "I don't understand this," "I'm dumb, I can't do this"), then you need to put in place processes and structures that ensure they have to ultimately do the work.

As well, whichever way you choose to discipline a student for undesirable behaviors, always use *the lightest touch necessary* to accomplish the change in behavior you are seeking. For example, never yell when a whisper will give you the result you are hoping to achieve.

This is the *principle of minimal intervention*—doing the least action necessary to bring about the change in behavior you want. Use the lightest touch necessary to bring about the desired change in behavior.

Remember the axiom: *there is nothing stronger than gentleness.*

And you also need to remember: *it is easier to move an elephant with a handful of peanuts than a big stick.*

Once your students like you and respect you, you will find that it doesn't take much to gain their cooperation.

By the way: Here is an example of a statement heard in most schools in North America each year. Teacher A, complaining about the students' behaviors, says, "I'm the teacher and they're the students. My job is to teach; their job is to listen and do what I tell them to do!" And with an attitude like that, such teachers just can't seem to figure out why the kids don't like them and why they have significant discipline problems on a daily basis.

It seems that teachers like this only want to teach "the good kids"—the kids who come to school neat, clean, and eager to learn. But this is like saying, "I want to be a doctor, but I don't want to treat any patients who are sick. I only want healthy people coming to my office." As a teacher, you have to take what walks through the classroom door—what I like to call, "The good . . . and the not yet good!"

It is highly probable that you will come across some students who—in spite of your best efforts—remain defiant and who regularly challenge you. While it is difficult to like these students, they do present opportunities for you. You can view them as "gifts" to you, as *your* teachers. Some will teach you patience. Some will teach you hope. Others will teach you humility. The way you treat with them will teach you a great deal about yourself.

In his book *Dream Class*, Michael Linsin (2014) describes five guidelines he followed when dealing with challenging students: "1) I treat them respectfully—even kindly; 2) I don't criticize personally or lecture them; 3) I don't talk to them more than I do other students; 4) I don't hold a grudge; and 5) I do exactly what I say I will do." There is some pretty good advice here for you as a teacher.

Linsin goes on to say that in regard to challenging students, "Few of them have ever been dealt with in this manner, and they appreciate it. It allows me to demand impeccable behavior without creating friction between us. Afterward, when they have fulfilled all of their obligations, I invite them back to be a part of the class with open arms. I am clear with all students, however, that our classroom is a special place, and anyone who upsets its harmony is not welcome."

Your classroom too ought to be a special place, and anyone who upsets its harmony should not be welcomed.

45. YOU DON'T WANT TO SEND KIDS TO THE PRINCIPAL'S OFFICE—AT LEAST, NOT OFTEN

It remains a mystery where teachers learn this, but many of them think that the ultimate threat they can utter in the classroom (usually in a loud, angry voice) is, "If you don't stop doing that, I'm going to send you to the principal's office!"

There are two significant problems with this course of action.

First, your principal is not likely to be too pleased with this discipline strategy of yours. Most principals are busy, and good principals are very busy.

They have their own responsibilities to contend with each day, and *doing your classroom discipline for you is not one of them.*

You will want to have a conversation very early in the school year with your administration to determine what types of discipline issues they want to be involved in and what types of discipline issues they see as your responsibility—and yours alone.

The second problem with this approach is the message it sends to the students in your class.

When you say to your students, "If you don't stop doing that, I'm going to send you to the principal's office!" what you are in effect saying is, "I can't deal with you. I need the principal to help me because I am too weak and don't have enough power to deal with this on my own."

You're essentially telling your students that you can't handle them. They will hear that message loudly and clearly—and so will your principal.

You are the classroom teacher. *You* are responsible for classroom management in your classroom—not the principal.

Sending a student to the office is an extreme measure and should therefore happen only in the most extreme situations.

By the way: If you find yourself in such an extreme situation (the kind of situation that really warrants sending a student to the principal's office), it is highly recommended that you never *send* a student to the office. Either *phone* the principal and describe the situation, or *take* the student yourself. Get a colleague to look in on your classroom and go to the office *with the student.* If you don't, the principal will have only the student's version of the story as to why he or she was sent to the office.

And one thing is certain: the student's story and your story will be different.

46. WHEN YOU BRING A PROBLEM TO YOUR PRINCIPAL, ALWAYS BRING A SOLUTION

OK, so you have an extreme situation, and you have chosen to bring a student to the office. How best to do this?

You *never* want to bring your principal a problem without bringing him or her at least one solution to the problem (two is even better). This applies not only to discipline problems that you might need the principal's help with but also to other kinds of problems that you may be having in regard to your work at school.

For example, you determine that you want to take your students on a field trip, but the trip costs more than your budgeted amount for field trips. Or perhaps it is only spring, and your printing allocation for the year is close to being maximized. Perhaps you want to purchase some additional resources for your classroom and want to access additional school funds.

Whatever issue or problem you bring to your principal, it is wise to bring at least one viable solution to present along with the problem.

If you have chosen to bring a student to the principal for assistance with discipline, you will want to propose some recommendations to the principal in regard to what you think will work best in this particular situation for this particular student.

It is important to keep in mind that the principal will probably not know the student as well as you do (if at all), and as a result she/he may be looking for some guidance in this situation. Different consequences work differently with different students—and the principal may not know what is likely to work best with this particular student. As this student's teacher, you should know this, and you should be able to make some recommendations to your principal in this regard.

As well, if bringing a student to the office is something that you do rarely, your principal is much more likely to take this situation seriously than if this is something you attempt to do on a regular basis.

In summary, do not bring discipline situations to your principal often; do not send a student to the principal—bring the student instead, or at the very least, call the principal or his or her administrative assistant and inform about the situation and that a student is on the way to the office. And again, always have at least one recommended solution to the problem you are presenting.

If you do this, both your principal and your students will respect you even more.

47. WHEN YOUR STUDENTS TELL YOU STORIES ABOUT THEIR FAMILIES

Most people love stories. We love to listen to them; we love to tell them. Your students are no different—they too will love to tell stories.

However, when they are young, their social filters are not yet well developed, and they will often say whatever is on their minds without thinking all that much about how the story portrays those being described in the story.

This applies especially to stories being told about their families.

As they get older, students tend to become more guarded about telling teachers stories that give their teachers a glimpse into their world outside of the classroom, but young students rarely have such filters.

While students—especially young students—may be eager to tell you stories about their life outside of school and what is going on at home, as a teacher, you need to be cautious in this circumstance and remember a couple of things.

First, if an eight-year-old child is telling you a story about something that happened at home, you are hearing these events as *experienced by an eight-year-old—through eight-year-old eyes and filtered through an eight-year-old brain*. While this is certainly one perspective—and perhaps a very valid one for the eight-year-old—you can be assured that an adult who witnessed these same events is most likely to have a different interpretation as to what is really going on.

Second, even in light of the above, it is important that—when appropriate—you listen attentively and empathetically to your students when they tell you stories about what is going on at home. They will want to feel respected and important, and listening carefully to them helps establish this.

However, you still need to be cautious. Please do not pass judgment or believe their stories "whole hog" without some degree of verification. This is particularly important in cases where the child may be telling stories about things going on in the home that may seem rather peculiar or potentially illegal. If this happens to you, seek guidance from your administration.

And always keep in mind, this "telling stories" is a road with two lanes—it goes both ways. While the child will be telling you stories about what happened at home, they are also telling their parent/caregivers stories about what happened at school.

You would be wise to make a pact with all of the parents/caregivers of your students at the beginning of each school year. Talk to them at your "meet the teacher night" and with a smile say, "I will agree *not* to believe everything your child tells me about what is going on in your home if *you* will agree not to believe everything your child tells you about what is going on in my classroom without checking with me first. Call me or e-mail me if you have any questions and we can clarify what's happening."

This pact will work well for you, your parents/caregivers, and your students.

By the way: One of the issues you will have to come to terms with is how much you should tell your students about *you* and *your personal life*. Some—if not most—of your students will be somewhat curious about who you are, where you came from, why you wanted to be a teacher, and so on. Some will have googled you.

There is a balance to be struck in terms of how much you tell them about your life outside of school, one that you will have to find for yourself. Having said that, however, there are times when revealing personal aspects about your life can be very helpful in winning students over.

For example, several years ago, I was sent to a relatively tough junior high school in the middle of the school year. The kids were already well established in their routines and behaviors—routines and behaviors that were not very conducive to teaching and learning. I was working hard to win them over and to establish more productive routines in our classroom, but I found this to be a hard struggle given that I was starting mid-year and not in September.

One day, I came to class with a very large chocolate Easter Bunny, and I asked the class, "Who likes chocolate?" and proceeded to break pieces off the bunny and give them to my students. They asked, "Where did you get the chocolate rabbit?" I replied, "My mom just stopped by the school and gave it to me. She lives not too far away, and she goes for long walks each day. Today she came by and gave me this bunny. Too much chocolate for just me."

The kids laughed. Here I was, a forty-plus-year-old man, and my mother was still giving me chocolate Easter Bunnies at Easter. The students thought this was hilarious—and so did I. We all shared a laugh, shared some chocolate, and then got to work.

Something changed after that. The kids were less defiant and a little more pleasant. I believe that it was because in the sharing of the chocolate and the telling the story about my mom, the kids began—for the first time—to see me as a real person; someone with a mom who loved him, someone who would share chocolate with them, and someone who could laugh at himself along with them.

You too will have opportunities to share personal aspects of your life with your students. Share the stories that will help you build relationships with your students, relationships that help you move toward a better learning environment in your classroom.

48. HOW TO GET PARENTS/CAREGIVERS TO LOOK FORWARD TO YOUR PHONE CALLS

In most cases, establishing an effective working relationship with a student's parents/caregivers will help you to be a more effective teacher with your students. Given this, it is important that you work to establish a good relationship with them whenever this is possible.

Now, take a step back from your role as a teacher and ask yourself this question: *What is it that most parents/caregivers want for their kids in school, and how can you give that to them?* A great question!

What most parents want is relatively simple: they want their kids to be *safe* at school; they want their kids to be *happy* at school; and they want their kids to *learn* at school. These are not unreasonable things for parent/caregivers to want.

There are two questions for you inherent in these parental/caregiver wishes.

First, *how* can you—as the teacher—establish an environment in your classroom where your students feel safe, happy, and they are learning?

The second question (one often neglected by teachers) is this: Once you have *established* these things, how do you *communicate* this to the parents/

caregivers of your students? How do you let them know that their child is safe, happy, and learning?

Keeping this a secret does not serve you well. You really ought to let the parents/caregivers in on the good news.

One mistake that many teachers make—from novice to veteran educators—is how, when, and on what occasions they make "the phone call home."

Many teachers phone home only when there is a problem with a student, when the student has misbehaved or failed to do assigned work. It is little wonder then that when the phone rings and whoever answers calls out to the parents/caregivers, "It's the school calling about Johnny" that when the parents/caregivers comes to the phone, they sound defensive.

If the only time you as a teacher call home is when the student is in trouble, what else do you expect but a defensive reaction?

It is a wise teacher who turns this all-too-typical situation upside down.

Teachers who want *positive relationships* with students and their parents/caregivers make *positive phone calls home*.

One way to do this is once a week, choose three or four students who have done something particularly well in your class that week (it could be school work related; it could be behavioral) and then phone home to tell the parents/caregivers the story.

You may want to speak to the student before talking to their parents/caregivers. The dialogue can go something like this:

You: Is Johnny home? It's [your name here] calling from the school.

Person who answered the phone, if it is a sibling (usually yelling): Johnny, it's the school calling. You're in trouble.

Johnny: Hello.

You: Hi Johnny. I'm phoning to tell your mom/dad/caregiver about (describe great behavior here), and I want you to put them on the phone after you and I have talked. I am telling you this so you know that when they get off the phone, they will likely be very pleased with you—maybe even shocked. This is a great opportunity for you, and you may want to use it in some way. Perhaps there is something you want from them. After this call might be a good time to ask. Just saying! I wanted to let you know that I am proud of what you did. My compliments! Now—may I please speak to. . . "

You would then proceed to tell mom/dad/caregiver about whatever great thing Johnny had done in your class that week.

When you do this early in the year, most of the parents/caregivers will be quite astonished at this kind of phone call. This is likely the first positive phone call they have ever received from a school (a sad testament to what most teachers do—but true nonetheless).

However, if you make these positive calls home consistently throughout the school year, when the time comes that you have to phone home to deal with a problem regarding a student, the experience is much more likely to result in an agreement with the parent/caregiver that resolves the issue.

You may think: "I don't have time to do this." You are wrong. If you make just *three positive calls home each week*—each one taking less than five minutes—you will have called the home of every student in your classroom in approximately two months, or four to five times for each student by the end of the school year.

Not a lot of time for such a huge payoff—for both you and your students.

By the way: Don't make these positive calls home during the school day— make them in the evenings or on the weekends. You are then much more likely to find the parents/caregiver(s) at home, and if you call at then, they will be even more impressed with your commitment to their children's success at school, given that you are calling on your own time—and rightly so.

49. PARENTS/CAREGIVERS AND E-MAILS: MANAGING EXPECTATIONS

Another way to establish great relations with the parents/caregivers of your students is to manage their expectations appropriately. This is particularly important when it comes to communication via e-mails or via the school's website.

Today, many schools have their own websites, and these sites usually list the names of all of the staff and their school e-mail addresses. This makes it easy and convenient for parents to communicate with you via e-mail.

That is generally a good thing. However, you need to be careful in regard to both the content and the timing of your e-mails.

First, the content. E-mailing parents/caregivers is not the same as texting or e-mailing your friends. When you e-mail a parent/caregiver, you are creating a permanent digital record of your communications. This is not the time to be humorous, sarcastic, overly critical, or to type like you text. Keep these communications brief, on point, and professional.

Second, the timing. Be very careful with the timing of your replies to parent/caregiver e-mails. Your job during the school day is to teach and work with students—not to respond to e-mails. While it may be tempting to check your e-mails during your prep period or at lunch or recess, if you choose to do this, do *not* respond to parents'/caregivers' e-mails during the school day.

Here's why. Imagine Ms. Baker e-mails you at 10:00 a.m. You have a prep at 10:30 a.m., and you reply to her at that time. Ms. Baker is impressed with

"*I want to tell you something really great your kid did at school this week!*"

Figure 3.4.

your prompt reply, and you feel good because this is now one more thing off of your "to do list" for that day.

The problem you have created by doing this is one of *expectations*. When Ms. Baker e-mails you early one morning a few weeks later, you have already established an expectation that she is going to receive a prompt response. When she hasn't heard from you by the afternoon, she may feel she is being ignored and that you are being rude and disrespectful.

One way to avoid this that will work for you and for the parents/caregivers is to manage the pressures of e-mail by making an e-mail schedule early in the school year—then sticking to it. Do *not* look at parents/caregivers e-mails sporadically and randomly throughout the day, and certainly *do not reply* to them at those times.

Instead, read parents/caregivers e-mails *once* a day (e.g., before or after classes) or twice a day (say before and after classes), but in either case, *set aside specific times to read and respond to e-mails and stick to those times*.

Inform your parents/caregivers at the beginning of the school year when they can expect to receive replies to their e-mails, then do not deviate from this. Let them know that in cases of emergency, they should phone the school rather than e-mailing you. You can communicate this in your opening letter to your parents/ caregivers as well as inform them of this during the "meet the teacher night."

There will be no unrealistic expectations established, you can spend your day focused on your students, and there will be no hurt feelings because parents/caregivers are feeling ignored.

By doing this, you will have established an effective communications strategy that can work for you, your students, and your parent/caregivers—a win-win for all.

50. DON'T CONFUSE ACTIVITY WITH ACHIEVEMENT

A number of years ago when I was teaching elementary school, the study of historical Greece was a major component of the social studies curriculum.

The curriculum was very explicit in terms of what aspects of Greece were to be explored. We were to examine concepts such as the birth of democracy, who had the right to vote and who was excluded, who had decision-making power in a society and on what basis, gender inequality, and so on.

I really enjoyed exploring these topics with my Grade 6 students. They were difficult concepts for eleven- and twelve-year-olds, but I found that when I brought them to life in our classroom by forming a class government based on ancient Greek ideas compared to modern liberal democratic ideas, well, "things got real" and the kids became quite involved.

It was hard work, required some creativity on my part, but my students and I worked through it together.

Across the hall, in the other Grade 6 classroom, my colleague chose a different approach to the topic of ancient Greece.

Her students built dioramas of the Parthenon. They had a Greek food day where the kids brought in Greek salad and Greek yogurt and had a Greek lunch. They had a toga and sword day where the kids put on old sheets and wore paper-mache helmets they had made and had battles with cardboard swords.

Figure 3.5.

Her kids loved it. Her class was very busy, and her students were having a great deal of fun. Just one problem.

Her students were *not* learning the curriculum, and she was *not* teaching the curriculum.

While the activities that were going on in her classroom were certainly *about* Greece, they were *not* about the prescribed curriculum. They were not about ancient Greece and the birth of democracy, and they did not explore the various concepts and questions in the curriculum around how best to govern a society.

The lesson here? When you teach, *do not confuse activity with achievement.*

It's not too difficult to come up with engaging and creative ways to keep kids busy and ensure they are having fun. However, *these activities are of little use if they are not relevant to the curriculum.*

Achievement for a teacher comes from your students mastering the curriculum, from your students engaging with the curricular concepts in ways that enhance their learning and understanding of the world. This does not imply that you can't have fun doing this learning work. Quite the opposite—in most classes learning should be fun, and the line between work and play in class should be very fuzzy.

It really is quite amazing to see how much students can learn while having fun at the same time.

51. WHAT DO YOU MEAN YOU ONLY TAUGHT THAT ONCE? THE NINE LAWS OF LEARNING

Many states and provinces have what are sometimes referred to as "high-stakes tests"—tests that students must write where the consequences of success or failure on these assessments is of significant consequence.

In the United States, there are almost 100 colleges and universities that either require or recommend SAT scores for consideration in determining admissions. In Canada, some provinces have major cumulative examinations at the end of high school, and the results of these exams are of major significance in determining whether or not a student is granted admission into university.

In some provinces in Canada, students are required to write diploma exams at the end of their Grade 12 year. The diploma exams are used as part of the criteria for admission into post-secondary institutions, so these exams—like the SATs in the United States—are of significant importance to any student seeking university or college admission.

Because of this, there is a great deal of pressure on teachers who teach diploma courses. They are expected to be a master of the material and to be able to help their students through the diploma exams successfully. This is important to the students, to their parents, and to the school administration.

After these exams are written and scored by the government, schools are provided with an exam analysis. It shows the teachers how each student responded to each of the exam items, and then it gives you an overall analysis. From this information, it is very easy to determine how your students performed on each item of the exam.

I recall a meeting with my high school social studies colleagues during which time we were reviewing how our students had performed on these diploma exams.

One teacher—whose students had not done well on this particular diploma exam—kept repeating, "I taught that. I don't know why they did so poorly on that question. I taught that!"

"How many times?" I asked.

"Once!" he replied, the expression on his face demonstrating that he really didn't understand my question.

John Wooden would not have approved of that response. Wooden coached basketball at the University of California, Los Angeles (UCLA), for many years. In a twelve-year period, Wooden and his UCLA team won ten NCAA national championships. To date, no other team has ever won more than two championships in a row.

Wooden was revered by his players, not only for his ability to teach them about basketball, but also for his ability to teach them about life.

Wooden was a master teacher. According to him, there are *nine laws of learning*, and he used them in his teaching. They are *explanation, demonstration, imitation, application, repetition, repetition, repetition, repetition, repetition.*

While you may not have the time in your classroom to repeat everything you teach five times as Wooden suggests in his laws of learning, *do not be under the illusion that because you have taught something once, your students have now learned it.*

Repetition is a powerful teaching tool, one that great teachers use with remarkable effectiveness in their classrooms, and you should too.

Let me say that again: Repetition is a powerful teaching tool, one that great teachers use with great effectiveness in their classrooms, and you should too.

Now, repeat after me. . .

By the way: You may find yourself feeling a great deal of pressure to "cover the curriculum" for the grade and subjects you teach, and thus be reluctant to do a lot of repetition in your classroom. However, you need to keep this in mind: if you are delivering the curriculum at such a fast pace or with such difficult content that your students are not really learning it, you might as well be in front of a mirror teaching yourself. It may look good—but there is no real learning going on.

52. IN PURSUIT OF PEPPERMINTS AND PEZ

As a teacher, you will continually have to deal with student behaviors—some good, some less so.

One school of thought regarding ways to influence human behavior is behavior modification theory. Basically, this psychology focuses on ways to motivate students to behave in certain ways by giving them positive reinforcements or negative consequences—a kind of "carrot and stick" approach to student discipline.

While many teachers do not generally support this approach as a way to get "kids to behave" (as discussed earlier, they have found building good relationships to be much more effective in the long term), you can still use this type of strategy on occasion to motivate kids and have a little fun at the same time.

I once had an old toilet come into my possession, and I happened to be teaching in an inner-city junior high school at the time. My kids were great, but it was a bit of a challenge to get some of them motivated to do the work.

Was there a way I could use this toilet in my teaching I wondered?

I spray-painted the toilet gold, and it appeared on top of my filing cabinets one Monday morning as the kids walked into my classroom. Naturally, they were curious—one doesn't often see a golden toilet on top of a filing cabinet in a classroom.

"Why is that toilet up there?" they asked.

"That's not a toilet—that's a *Pot of Gold*!" I replied with a smile.

I told them that from then on, I would be passing out gold slips at random when kids were on task. They were to put their names on these slips and in a phrase describe what they were doing at the exact time I gave them the gold slip (this would be some kind of behavior that I was trying to reinforce). They were to then put their gold slip into the Pot of Gold. I would then draw these slips out of our Pot of Gold, and the winners would receive prizes—some prizes were for individuals while some were for the whole class. I told them I would do this at the end of each week (for quick reinforcement). I made a "prize poster," and each Monday I would display that week's prizes that would be drawn for every Friday.

We had a lot of fun with this, and more kids were on task more frequently as a result.

There was a teacher who taught junior high school math, and he used a PEZ candy dispenser on occasion to shoot out candies to students who performed well on fun little math exercises. There were thirty teenagers highly engaged in math activities—all in the hopes of winning a PEZ.

In high school, another teacher did something similar with peppermints. He would have a jar of peppermints at the front of the room, and once or twice a week he would have social studies trivia contests related to what the class had studied that week. Three correct answers and a student won a peppermint.

Please understand, the peppermint was worth about one cent. Many of these kids came from fairly affluent families. Several of them had part-time jobs, drove their own cars, and had a fair amount of disposable income of their own.

Yet, even with all of that, they engaged in the "Pursuit of Peppermints" game with an unrelenting focus on winning. At first it can be difficult to understand why they were so intent on winning. Think about it. *The real prize was not the peppermint—the real prize was the win.*

Be creative in the ways you motivate your students, and make it fun—for both them and you. And remember, you can reward your students for all kinds of different achievements besides those that are academic. You can reward and recognize them for things like most organized, most improved, most creative, most kind, and the list goes on.

Having said that, however, you need to be judicious in how you reward your students, and for what quality of work. If you reward students constantly for work that is far less than they are capable of producing, you are sending them a message that minimal effort is praiseworthy and satisfactory work is good enough. You will want to carefully consider when and how you reward students, and for what quality of work.

By the way: Ultimately, while these kinds of extrinsic reward systems can be a lot of fun and can certainly be effective in motivating many students to engage in learning, eventually—when you become more experienced—you will likely find yourself moving beyond these types of reward systems.

These extrinsic reward systems are a good place to *start*, but they are not where you want to *end*. Eventually, you want to get your students to a place where they come to see that knowledge has value, that learning can be a lot of fun, that it is wonderful to be curious about something, and then to embark upon a journey to satisfy their curiosity.

All of these kinds of rewards are *intrinsic*, and it ought to be our ultimate goal as teachers to get our students to a place where there is joy and accomplishment in the learning itself.

53. SO YOU REACHED THE END OF SEPTEMBER—TIME TO TAKE A GOOD LOOK AROUND YOU

You will often hear master teachers say, "If you don't have your students where you want them by the end of September, you won't ever get them there. You've lost them, and it is going to be a very long and very difficult year for you as a teacher!" This is a great truth about teaching.

At the end of your first September, you need to take a very close look at what has happened in your classroom over the first month of school. You need to explore answers to questions such as the following:

1. What kind of *relationship* do you have with your students—both individually and with the class or classes as a whole?
2. What kinds of *routines* are in place in your classroom? Are there procedures that work well and have become effective routines in your classroom? Are there procedures that you need to tweak because they aren't working so well?
3. Have you "set the stage" properly with your students so that you and your students are very likely to have a great school year in your classroom—a

year filled with fun, learning, productive work, and substantial student growth?

If your answer is "Yes" to most—if not all—of these questions, you are well on your way to a wonderful school year. Congratulations!

If your answer is "No" to any of these question, you have a lot of work to do. Get started on that work very, very quickly (that means *now!*)—time is getting wasted.

Section Four

What You Need to Do during the Rest of the Year

INTRODUCTION

At this stage, you have reached the end of September, and things are going quite well. You know your students well enough to teach them rather effectively; you have good relationships with most, if not all, of your students; you have the bulk of your classroom routines well established; and you think you are on your way to a fairly successful first year of teaching.

What should you work on next?

Now, and for the remainder of the year, you will want to pay particular attention to *refining your skills as a teacher*.

This section of this book will focus on showing you a variety of strategies you need to consider concerning your relationships with students, your teaching methods, and yourself as a teacher so that you can successfully navigate the remainder of the school year.

54. GREAT TEACHERS ARE GREAT STORYTELLERS WITH GREAT STORIES TO TELL

"No one ever made a decision because of a number. They need a story." Amos Tversky and Daniel Kahneman argued this point persuasively, and then went on to show that for the most part, human beings decide things emotionally, not rationally (the story of their remarkable work is told in the Michael Lewis (2017) book *The Undoing Project: A Friendship That Changed Our Minds*).

We love to tell stories; we love to hear stories. *Great teachers understand that stories are a wonderful way to teach*. Aesop knew the power of stories to teach over 2,000 years ago in ancient Greece. Stories work just as effectively in classrooms today—and great teachers use story to great effect.

Why is this? Because great stories touch us emotionally. Because the right story teaches students in ways that numbers and facts cannot. Because students inevitably insert themselves into the story. Students listen to the story and judge the actions of its characters. They think things such as: "I wouldn't have done that—that's not going to work. I would have done this—a far better choice!" We also relate to the characters in the stories: "Oh yeah, that reminds me of the time I. . . "

We do this as teachers, and so do our students. Stories serve as *windows* through which we can see the world in new ways. They also serve as *mirrors* by which we can see ourselves ever more fully and clearly.

Good stories well told capture the attention and interest of our students, and students then learn about the world and themselves through their reactions to what happens in these stories.

If you want to be a great teacher, you will collect great stories wherever you find them (books, YouTube, Facebook, TV, movies, personal experience, friends, family, comics, graphic novels, etc.), and you will learn when to use these stories and how to tell them effectively in order to capture the minds and hearts of your students and to teach them both curriculum and lessons about life.

All great teachers are great storytellers, and you can be one too!

55. REMEMBER THE STARFISH STORY—YOU CANNOT SAVE THEM ALL

A man was walking along a deserted beach at sunset. As he walked, he could see a young boy in the distance.

As he drew nearer, he noticed that the boy kept bending down, picking something up, and throwing it into the water. Time and again, the boy kept hurling things into the ocean.

As the man approached even closer, he was able to see that the boy was picking up starfish that had been washed up on the beach, and one at a time, he was throwing them back into the water.

The man asked the boy what he was doing. The young boy paused, looked up, and replied, "Throwing starfish into the ocean. The tide has washed them up onto the beach and they can't return to the sea by themselves. When the sun gets high, they will die unless I throw it back into the water."

"But," said the man, "you can't possibly save them all. There are thousands of starfish on this beach, and this must be happening on hundreds of beaches along the coast. You can't possibly make a difference."

The boy smiled, bent down, and picked up another starfish, and as he threw it back into the sea, he replied, "I made a difference to that one."

Adapted from: The Star Thrower by Loren Eiseley (1978)

There is a great lesson for you as a teacher in this story: *You cannot save them all. It is not your job to save them all.*

Figure 4.1.

ın becoming a teacher, you have entered into what Nell Noddings (1989) calls one of the "caring professions," professions whose primary mission is to help people. Medicine, nursing, and social work are other examples of caring professions.

Joan Halifax, a Zen abbot, cautions people in these kinds of professions about the dangers of trying to do too much on the road we travel in trying to do good. She calls these dangers "edge states," and she warns that qualities such as altruism, empathy, and engagement all have the potential—if we take them too far or engage in them inappropriately—to become self-destructive.

For example, as a teacher, your altruism can turn into what Halifax calls "pathological altruism" if you take it to extremes. Another example is where your empathy for some students may blind you to the actual reality of their lives and what they truly need.

As a teacher, you are working with students—a lot of students—and these students have *unlimited needs*, while you—their teacher—are a person with *limited time, limited energy*, and *limited resources*.

You cannot save them all (and try to remember, not all of them need saving). Do the very best you can, with what you have, where you are, and then be forgiving of yourself when you feel that you have come up short.

That is all you can do—and that is often more than enough.

56. YOU MUST LEARN TO ADJUST

There is a story told of a famous and accomplished actor who received a call one day from a movie producer friend. The producer wanted him to star in an upcoming film he was financing. The actor agreed.

A few days into shooting, the actor called his producer friend to complain about the film's director.

"He doesn't let me act the way I want to" complained the famous actor. "I have won academy awards, and he won't let me interpret the role the way I want to. He keeps bossing me around and making me do it his way!" the actor went on.

His producer friend listened quietly and then replied, "Darling, you must learn to adjust!"

Darling, you must learn to adjust! Teaching will *not* be what you thought it was going to be like when you were a college or university student. If you are an experienced teacher, you will have already seen several changes in terms of the teaching profession—changes in technology, changes in expectations of teachers, changes in curriculum, changes in students, and so on. *You must learn to adjust!*

Teaching will not be the way you remember it back when you were a student. Nor will teaching be like what some of your professors told you in university. Nor will it be like it was when you first started teaching. Teaching is in a constant state of flux.

You must learn to adjust—the school, the kids, the staff, and parents will not adjust for you.

Remember, universities and colleges are often quite liberal in their views, and they operate in a world that works with adults. School staffs and school boards, on the other hand, can be quite conservative in their views, and teachers operate in a world where their work is primarily with minor children. You will be expected to adjust to their ways and their world when you start teaching—they will not adjust to you.

As good as you think you are and as much as you think you know, schools and school systems will not adjust to you. Darling, *you* must learn to adjust.

57. NOT MY CIRCUS, NOT MY MONKEYS

Most teachers love to help people. It is a reflective response that is seen in all good teachers. Helping comes naturally to good teachers; it makes them feel useful, and it makes them feel good.

As a teacher, I have a poster at my desk that says: "Not my circus, not my monkeys." I have it there because it reminds me to constantly ask this question, a question you will want to ask of yourself as well.

When staff, students, and parents bring you problems and issues (and this happens a great deal in teaching)—and they want *you* to take these problems on and deal with them—you need to ask yourself: Is this really *your* problem? Is it appropriate that *you* get involved with this issue? Is it *your* responsibility to take this problem or task on? Is this something that will help *you* achieve your goals and mission as a teacher? In other words, "Whose problem is this—really?"

You too need to ask yourself these kinds of questions as the plethora of problems and demands comes at you throughout your many years of teaching. "Is this *really* your problem?"

If your answer is "Yes," then by all means get involved and do something about the situation.

However, sometimes the answer is "No—not my problem!" In other words, "Not my circus, not my monkeys."

That is the time to get back to what really matters.

Figure 4.2.

58. REMEMBER . . . THERE IS ALWAYS ENOUGH TIME TO DO THE MOST IMPORTANT THINGS

There will never be enough time to do everything you want to do as a teacher. As we discussed earlier, you are working in a profession where there are unlimited needs, but you have limited resources, limited energy, and limited time.

Having said that, however, you need to remember this: *there is always enough time to do the most important things.*

This is similar to the discussion we had earlier about putting first things first. If you can determine what the most essential things are for you to accomplish—the *things you must do in order for you to be a successful teacher*—then you can work hard to ensure that these things get done.

You can always choose to give the important things in teaching the time, focus, and energy they need and to ignore or minimize the multitude of interruptions and distractions that are a part of every teacher's day.

Put *your* teaching priorities first. Your teaching priorities are where you should find yourself spending most of your time and most of your energy.

Spend the majority of your time on your priorities, the things that are the most important to you in your quest to become a great teacher. You will find there is always enough time for those.

By the way: Obviously, before you can put "first things first" and truly focus on your priorities as a teacher, you need to discern what those priorities truly are. In order to do that, you must first answer *the vision question,* which asks: *What would your classroom look like if everything was ideal?* It is important to recognize here that you will never achieve your vision, and achieving your vision is not the point. The point is to be moving closer toward it day after day. Again, please remember: *the goal is progress, not perfection.* Make a list of at least ten ways your classroom would look if everything was perfect.

Next, answer *the mission question.* Your mission is your attempt to answer questions such as: What are you going to do to move toward your vision of an ideal classroom? Why do you do the work that you do—what is your fundamental purpose for teaching your students? What do you hope to achieve?

The mission of most teachers in general terms is to make a difference in the lives of their students and to help their students develop and grow into happy, contributing members of society. Each teacher does this in his or her own way, and thus your answer to the mission question will be particular to you and the students you are working with.

Once you answer your vision and mission questions, you have discovered your priorities as a teacher. You will know what needs to come first. Your task now is to work diligently to keep "first things first."

59. LEARN TO MAKE STAFF MEETINGS PRODUCTIVE

A great truth about teachers is that most teachers do not like staff meetings. The reason that the majority of teachers dislike staff meetings is that staff meetings are seen by many teachers as being a waste of valuable time.

In schools throughout the country, teachers lament, "The principal could have just sent all of that information in an e-mail. This meeting was a waste of my time." And unfortunately, often they are right.

What can you do about this? What can you do to ensure that staff meetings are *not* a waste of time for you?

You can do this by bringing work to a staff meeting. Marking is best. That way, no matter how long, boring, or irrelevant the particular agenda topic may be for you, staff meeting time is guaranteed to be productive time for you.

Instead of leaving the meeting frustrated, you will have bought yourself a free evening because your prep work or marking will already be completed by the time the staff meeting is over. Win-win!

By the way: You need to be respectful and discrete in following this advice. You don't want to antagonize your principal by seeming to ignore him or her during staff meetings. However, it is likely you will find that as long as you are paying attention and are respectful and engage appropriately in the discussions, many principals will understand what you are doing and why you are doing it and would view your marking during staff meetings as a good use of your time.

60. LEARN TO SAY "NO" NICELY

In an interview with *Business Week* in 2004, Steve Jobs said: "It comes from saying no to 1,000 things to make sure we don't get on the wrong track or try to do too much. We're always thinking about new markets we could enter, but *it's only by saying no that you can concentrate on the things that are really important* (http://www.bbc.co.uk/news/mobile/world-us-canada-15195448, Emphasis added)."

To repeat: "It's only by saying no that you can concentrate on the things that are really important."

As a teacher, there will be a lot of demands placed on you. Many of these will be mandatory—things you simply have to do because they are a part of the job.

However, you will also find that you will be asked to become involved in a number of activities that are in fact *optional*. They are not a mandatory part of the work, but rather projects that kids and colleagues and perhaps even parents/caregivers invite you to be a part of, activities such as committee work, coaching, and clubs.

Be very careful here! Committees, coaching, and clubs can be a lot of fun and are an excellent way to get to know kids and colleagues in a different way. However, they can also take up a great deal of time and energy—two resources that you will find in very short supply as a teacher.

Do not be afraid to say, "No, thank you." This will be especially important in your first years of teaching or any time you change grades or schools or the curriculum changes. You are already going to be extremely busy learning new curriculum, preparing, assessing, and refining your teaching skills. These ought to be your first priority, and you need to avoid getting involved in too many projects that take you away from what should be the center of your attention—your kids, your curriculum, your classroom, and your mission.

As a teacher, you are serving others, and you need to recognize that when you are serving others, taking good care of yourself is extremely important. If you try to please everyone with a continual parade of "Yes" to every request, it is very likely that you will suffer from fatigue, possible burnout, and frustration caused by doing many things poorly. And most certainly, your classroom teaching (which should always be the first priority of your work) will suffer as well.

In order to accomplish this, you will need to be very judicious in determining what activities you choose to get involved in outside of the classroom and outside of the school. Again a reminder: you have limited time, limited energy, and limited resources. You will need to spend these wisely.

You need to learn how to say "No, thank you" in a nice way. Here's a suggestion; go to a mirror, look at yourself and repeat one of the following phrases ten times:

- "Thanks, but I'm just too busy at this time."
- "Thanks for thinking of me, maybe next year."
- "I would love to get involved in that, but not this year. My kids and my classroom have to come first."

Steve Jobs also said, "Focusing is about saying no." If you are truly going to focus on your classroom, you are going to have to learn to say "No" to many of the requests that will come your way.

There is a story I was told about a teacher who had a sign by his phone that stated, "I said *no* today, and I don't feel guilty!" There is some good mental health in this for you.

61. MAKE THE 80–20 RULE WORK FOR YOU

Pareto's Principle—aka "the 80–20 rule"—states that for many activities, approximately 80 percent of the results we achieve come from 20 percent of our efforts.

In 1896, Italian economist Vilfredo Pareto published a paper showing that approximately 80 percent of the land in Italy was owned by 20 percent of the population. Pareto then further developed the principle by noting that 20 percent of the peapods in his garden contained 80 percent of the peas.

Pareto's "80–20 rule" has been found to apply to many things. For example, if you were to take a look in your closet, you would find that generally, you wear 20 percent of your clothes 80 percent of the time. Professional house painters have told me that painting a room is 20 percent actual painting and 80 percent prep work. Most teachers would readily tell you that 20 percent of their students take 80 percent of their efforts. This is Pareto's Principle at work.

So, how can this knowledge help you in your teaching?

You will likely see—if you look closely enough—that approximately 80 percent of your results will come from 20 percent of your efforts.

The challenge is to figure out the answer to this question: *What teaching activities are you engaged in (Is it your lesson planning, your actual teaching, your assessment strategies, your relationships with your students, your professional development projects, and so on?) that give you the greatest results in terms of your students' learning?* Is it one or two of these undertakings? Is it an appropriate blend of all of them, and if so—what is the best blend?

Teaching is very complex, and you simply cannot do *everything* well. But all of us can do a few things well. Pareto's Principle is telling you that you ought to think long and hard to figure out exactly what those few things are, and then do those things that will make the most significant difference to your success as a teacher—success that ultimately shows itself in the form of student learning.

This will not be an easy thing to do. It is difficult to figure out where we can get our "biggest bang for the buck"—and this is true for any occupation, but perhaps more so for teachers.

Teaching is often, unfortunately, very fad oriented. There are new "silver bullets" that come along all too frequently, and you may find yourself being encouraged (or perhaps even pressured) into learning about and adopting these new strategies, methods, techniques, technologies, or resources.

Be very careful when this happens. If you chase after every new fad that comes along in education—searching for the one new thing that will virtually guarantee cooperative students who learn in your classroom—you will likely find yourself unhappy, frustrated, and disappointed.

Instead, when you can successfully answer the question about what things you do well that have the greatest impact on your students' learning, then you will have figured out how best to spend your time and where best to spend your energy in order to get the best results for you—and for your students.

62. BECOME FIRST A GOOD ANIMAL

In his book *Running and Being*, George Sheehan (1978) paraphrases Ralph Waldo Emmerson and advises his readers to "become first a good animal." Sheehan was a medical doctor and long-distance runner who wrote for the magazine *Runner's World*. Sheehan argued that most human beings forget that we are first a kind of animal, and like all animals, we need to take care of ourselves physically. We need to tend to our bodies as well as to our minds. We can—and often do—lose sight of this in our quests to advance ourselves financially, intellectually, spiritually, and so on.

Good teaching is very demanding—both emotionally and physically. Yet, you cannot take proper care of others if you allow yourself to get run down physically. You simply will not have the energy. As Stephen Covey (1989) said in *The Seven Habits of Highly Effective People*, we must take time out to "sharpen the saw" if we intend to keep cutting wood.

This is similar to the tale of the woman and the woodcutter. Once upon a time, a woman was walking down the road near her home, and she came across a man attempting to cut down a very large tree. They said hello to one another, but the man quickly went back to his chopping, telling the woman that he wanted to get the job finished before the sun when down. The woman watched for a short while and then went on her way home. A couple of hours later, she returned with a large bottle of water and a sharpening stone.

The man was still chopping away intensely, breathing heavily, sweat running off his face. "Sir," she said, "I think you might be better off taking a small break to catch your breath, have a drink of water, and perhaps sharpen your axe, which appears to be very dull." The man snapped at her, "Go away woman. I don't have time for that!"

As a teacher, it is crucial that you take care of your body physically. You really ought to have a good breakfast, stay hydrated all day, snack every three hours of the school day to keep your blood sugar balanced, and get enough sleep. All of these are crucial because teaching is very demanding: intellectually, emotionally, *and physically*, and if you are going to keep up to the physical demands of teaching, good physical health habits are essential.

As well, you will want to nurture your mind with good conversation, good books, good movies, meditation, and prayer—whatever works for you.

You need to stay physically and mentally healthy in order to keep up the pace, the intensity, and the awareness that good teaching requires.

If you do not take time out to "sharpen the saw"—that is, take time to take care of yourself physically, emotionally, and spiritually—you will all too soon find yourself feeling run down, ill, irritable, and impatient with your students. These are not the characteristics of great teachers.

So, please remember: *first, be a good animal!*

63. WHO DO YOU NEED TO FORGIVE THE MOST?

There is a story told about the great teachers in history, one of whom was Jesus Christ. Jesus often used parables—short stories with life lessons contained therein, much like Aesop did with his fables—to make his point.

It is important to remember that according to the gospels, Christ is said to have walked on water, raised the dead, and turned water into wine. Jesus was also a teacher. He had a 12–1 ratio, and even with that, *one failed.*

There is a lesson in this story for you.

Along the lines of the starfish story mentioned earlier, which stressed that it is not your job to save every student, you need to recognize that on occasion, some of your students will fail.

They will fail in a variety of ways. They will fail to attend class; they will fail to care; they will fail to see the consequences of their poor decisions; they will fail to see that you genuinely care about them; they will fail to participate; they will fail exams; and they may even fail to stay in school.

When this happens, you will need to be patient and forgiving of yourself.

You cannot save them all, and you are certainly not divine. You will make mistakes—lots of them. But you are a teacher, and you are a learner. And remember, you never lose when you learn the lesson.

All you can do is the best you can, with what you have, and where you are. If you can honestly look yourself in the mirror and say you have done that, then do not blame yourself for those students who fail at a particular time. For them, there is always tomorrow.

As for you their teacher, you can be at peace with yourself when you know you did your very best.

Again, a reminder, *the goal is progress, not perfection.*

64. IF YOUR NAME IS JOHNNY, YOU MUST BE BAD

Did you ever notice that most of the jokes about bad kids in school are about boys named Johnny, as in: "Johnny and his grade one class went on a field trip to a farm. . . "?

Names are interesting when you are a teacher. Not only is it important that we spell and pronounce our students' names correctly (and be willing to call a student by their preferred nickname—assuming the nickname is appropriate for public consumption), it is also important that we become aware of our biases regarding names.

This becomes increasingly important the longer you teach.

As we teach year after year, we will have experiences—both good and not so good—with students who have certain names. We may then begin to associate certain kinds of behaviors with certain students' names.

For example, if you have taught five students in the past who were named Billy, and four of these five students had discipline problems, you might tend to think—even unconsciously—that if you see a student named Billy on your class list for the upcoming year, this kid is likely to be a problem.

It is very easy at a conscious level to recognize how unfair this is to the upcoming Billy. It is not so easy to recognize and deal with this when it lurks at an unconscious level.

The opposite is also true. Imagine you have taught three students in the past who were named Jeanine, and they were all hardworking, pleasant, serious students who were goal oriented and eager to learn—an absolute delight to have in your class!

"Oh, I see I have a student next year named Jeanine. I bet she'll be excellent." You see the problem.

Our unconscious will certainly impact our relationship with our students. It is critical that you as a teacher try and be aware of this, especially if it is causing damage to your relationships with particular students.

It is not fair to them, and it prevents you from doing the best job you can.

65. I AM NOT MY OLDER BROTHER. . .

In #64, we explored the unconscious impact that names can have on us and how they can affect our relationships with students. This can also hold true for members of the same family.

If you have previously taught two students from the Jones family, and they were both exceptionally great students, and now you have the next "Jones kid" (let's call her Janet) in your class, what will you expect? If you're not careful, you will fail to see Janet as the unique person she is, and instead, you will see her as the stereotypical "Jones kid" that is in your mind—a student who will be exceptional and great to teach—just like her two older siblings.

This is both problematic for you and unfair to the student.

It is a problem for you and unfair to her because if you do this, you will fail to see Janet as the individual she is. She may turn out to be a great student, a problem student, a mediocre student, or a student who excels in some areas and not others. Whichever way she ultimately is in your classroom, *she is who she is—she is not her older siblings*.

You need to understand that and not prejudge her based on your experiences with her older brother and sister. To do so is blatantly unfair to

..—and a major impediment to you being able to teach her or build an effective working relationship with her in any kind of authentic way.

The same notion holds true if the older siblings have been a challenge to teach and you do not have good memories or feelings toward their family.

As a teacher, you need to take your students as the individuals they are. They are not their older siblings. She is not "Doug's little sister" nor is he "Marnie's little brother." They are who they are, so please accept them as such.

66. REMEMBER THIS ABOUT YOUR STUDENTS—THEY'RE NOT DONE YET

For those of you who do any baking (cakes, bread, banana loaves, and the like), you will be very aware of the importance that *time* plays in the endeavor of baking anything. You know that you need to give your baking enough time in the oven for it to bake to the point where it is properly done. Too much time, and it's burned. Too little time, and it's underbaked.

This applies to gardening as well. If you pull up the potatoes or carrots weeks before their proper time, they will be too small and will not have matured to their optimal size. If you pluck a rose too early and try to peel open the petals on the bud instead of letting them unfold in their own time, you simply damage the rose. You won't get a beautiful flower.

So too it is with your students.

Every student who comes to you drawing breath is *not done yet*. They are a work in progress, and that progress is in a constant state of change.

There is abundant evidence of this great truth for those of us who teach. *Chicken Soup for the Soul* has a chapter that describes some teachers' judgments of their students—students I think you will recognize.

- "Beethoven handled the violin awkwardly and preferred playing his own compositions instead of improving his technique. His teacher called him hopeless as a composer."
- In his autobiography, Charles Darwin wrote, "I was considered by all my masters [teachers] and by my father, a very ordinary boy, rather below the common standard in intellect."
- "Thomas Edison's teachers said he was too stupid to learn anything."
- Albert Einstein's teacher described him as "mentally slow, unsociable and adrift forever in his foolish dreams."
- "Leo Tolstoy, author of *War and Peace*, flunked out of college. He was described as 'both unable and unwilling to learn.'"
- Winston Churchill failed the sixth grade.

In his 2016 book *A Life in Parts*, Bryan Cranston (aka Walter White of *Breaking Bad* fame) describes his Grade 5 report card as filled with ominous statements: "Bryan needs to apply himself." "Bryan is often goofing around and disruptive. Bryan spends too much time daydreaming."

Figure 4.3.

These observations do not necessarily imply that all of these teachers were wrong in their assessments of students at the time they made them. That is not the point.

The point is that you—as a teacher—have the opportunity to work with your students for only a brief portion of their life's journey. They all have a past that they bring into your classroom, and they all have a future in which you will probably not play a part.

So please be patient with their faults, their flaws, and their failures. Be patient with what they do not yet know or are struggling unsuccessfully to learn from you. Remember, *they're not done yet*. This is not to say that you shouldn't have expectations for your students. However, your expectations— be they behavioral or academic—need to be age- or grade-level-appropriate. This fundamental truth about teaching seems to have escaped some in our profession.

It is bewildering to hear an elementary teacher criticizing and complaining about a seven-year-old who is acting like they are . . . well, seven years old. It is, as well, somewhat bewildering to hear a high school teacher criticizing and complaining about a seventeen-year-old who is acting like they are . . . seventeen.

It is unrealistic to expect your students to act with a maturity far beyond their years, because *they're not done yet*. For your students, there are more experiences to be had, more lessons to be learned, more life to be lived, and more maturing yet to come.

An elementary teacher told me the story of a group of Grade 4 boys who were goofing around in the back of his classroom. The teacher walked up to the boys and said in a firm voice, "Come on you guys, grow up!" One of the boys looked up at him, smiled, and said (with absolutely no hostility or defiance whatsoever), "We are growing up."

This teacher was wise enough to laugh and respond, "Well yes, you are."

So please don't judge your students too harshly or too soon. Remember, *they are still growing up. They're not done yet.*

67. YOU CAN'T FREE A FISH FROM WATER—YOUR STUDENTS LIVE AT HOME

If you google the phrase "You can't free a fish from water," you will discover that it originates from the TV series *Star Trek: Deep Space Nine*. This phrase is known as the Ferengi Rule of Acquisition #217. Who knew that the Ferengis have something of value to teach educators?

There is one immutable fact about teaching: unless you teach at a boarding school, your students do not live at school. They come from homes outside of school.

Figure 4.4.

These homes come in a variety of forms. Some will have a mom and dad; some will have blended families; some will have single parents; some will have LGBTQ+ parents/caregivers; some will have students being raised by grandparents; and some of your students will be in foster care or group homes run by the government. Some of these parents/caregivers will be kind and caring and nurturing, while others will be indifferent or worse yet—abusive in some ways.

As a teacher, you can disagree with the parents' or caregivers' values and how they are raising the kids who are in your class. Nonetheless, *you can't take your students home to live with you* because you think you could raise them better. Or, put another way, "You can't free a fish from water."

If you have a student whose home is not supportive of what you are trying to accomplish with that particular student and you can't get the parents/caregivers to support your efforts with their child, you really have no choice other than to work directly and only with the student. There really is no other option.

And, in cases such as these, you will likely be frustrated, disappointed, and discouraged.

Please don't take those feelings out on the student or give up on them. These kids need great teachers more than most.

I was registering new students at a Grade 7 to 9 school several years ago when a father came up to me and introduced his twelve-year-old son to me with these words, "This is Phil, *my little thief.* He will steal anything he can. Don't take your eyes off of this one."

As this father chuckled at his own words, I looked at this little boy, who could only stare down at the floor. Were his father's words a self-fulfilling prophecy? I wondered.

Working as a school principal, I once suspended a fourteen-year-old boy for fighting in school. He had beaten up another boy quite seriously. The father came to see me after school that day and yelled at me, "There are only two kinds of people in the world, hammers and nails, and I'm teaching my son to be a hammer!" Was it any wonder his son was violent?

In the film *The Help,* there is a scene where the housekeeper performs a daily ritual with the young girl in her care. She takes the child on her lap and says lovingly, "You is smart. You is kind. You is important." Who would be surprised to see this little girl grow to be a woman who is smart, kind, and important?

It is quite probable that all three of these children would live up to the image placed upon them by their parent/caregivers—one a thief; one physically violent; and one who will be smart and kind.

There is an old tale about a farmer who found an eagle's egg and decided to put it in the nest of one of his barnyard hens. The egg hatched, and the eagle grew up with the brood of chicks it had hatched with.

All of its life, this eagle did what the chickens did, because it thought it was a chicken. It scratched the earth, and ate seeds and worms. And when it attempted to fly, it could only fly a short distance—and low to the ground—just like the chickens could.

This eagle lived for many years in the barnyard, until it grew old. One day, while looking up to the sky, it saw a magnificent bird flying high in a cloudless sky.

"What kind of bird is that?" the eagle asked the chickens as it looked up in awe at the golden eagle soaring directly above.

"That's an eagle, the king of the birds," they replied. "He belongs to the sky because he is an eagle, and we belong to the earth because we're chickens."

This eagle lived and died as a chicken, because that is what it thought it was.

Once children absorb ideas about who and what they are—ideas they can get from caregivers, peers, teachers, and media—these notions of self-concept can be challenging to change, even if they are highly inaccurate.

Prescott Lecky was a lecturer of psychology at Columbia University from 1924 to 1934. Lecky developed what he called his "self-consistency theory," which basically said that each of us develops certain ideas about ourselves and we then work hard to maintain this self-image. This image, especially in younger people, can be greatly influenced by significant adults like teachers and parents. After extensive study with children, Lecky came to believe that *poor performance in school was almost always a direct result of a poor self-image.*

It is critical for us, as teachers, to recognize those students in our classrooms who have a poor self-image, and then to work hard and constantly to change this into something positive.

In an interview with *LIFE* magazine in 1965, educator Louis Johannot made a comment that received considerable attention, a comment that has an invaluable lesson for all educators. He said, "The only reason I always try to meet and know the parents better is because it helps me to forgive their children."

It is sometimes hard for us to accept this as teachers, but we need to understand that we are not in control of much beyond our classrooms when it comes to our students.

The most we can generally do is to make our classrooms good and nurturing places for our students during the time they are with us.

While you may not be able to "free the fish from the water" during the time you are teaching them, what you can do is show them that they have potential, that they are not always going to be stuck where they currently are. You can show them other possible futures and then give them the tools and tenacity they will need to make positive changes in their future once they have more control of their own lives.

You can see the potential and the promise in children that they may be unable to see for themselves. Show them their value and their possibilities over and over, in many different ways, so often and so persistently so that finally, they will be able to see it for themselves.

68. THEY ALREADY HAVE FRIENDS

When you first start your teaching career, especially if you start teaching in high school, you will not be much older than your students. As well, the memories of the times you were back in junior/high-middle school and high school are relatively fresh in your mind.

The students may see you as young and "cool"—far more "with it" than some of their older teachers. You may feel a kind of "connection" with your students, and in some ways, this may be because you see yourself as not so different from them. *But you are different. They are your students; you are their teacher.*

You may even find that your students encourage you to be friends with them. They may tell you things like "you're not like our other teachers" (aka the older teachers). This might feel good to you, but it is a temptation—not a compliment.

You can avoid this temptation by ensuring that you dress professionally, that you avoid deeply personal conversations with your students (send them to the school counselor if it is counseling they need), and that you act professionally.

The reality of teaching is that you will be required to act toward your students in ways that a friend would not. If you hear a student swearing or see them bullying another student, you must correct this behavior and have them deal with the consequences of their choice. A friend would be unlikely to do this, but you—as their teacher—must.

A while back, I was having a conversation with a young man in my Grade 12 class (a very smart and outgoing young man), and I was telling him how disappointed I was in him for not putting forth much effort on an important assignment. I told him I expected much more from him. He could tell I was serious and tried to lighten the mood and change the subject.

He looked at me, smiled his most charming smile, and said, "But Dr. Ripley— we're friends aren't we?"

I will give you my response and encourage you to use it in similar situations.

"Mr. Marko," I replied with a smile. "I have friends. You're *not* one of them. Maybe someday you and I will become friends—say in twenty or thirty years. But that is *not happening today.*"

He smiled and redid the assignment.

Remember, they have friends, and you are not—and should not be—one of them.

69. DO YOU WANT TO HEAR A JOKE?

After a few years of teaching, I thought I had figured out how to avoid most problems with students. I had made some mistakes, and I had learned from them. Therefore, when this little Grade 7 girl came up to me before class one morning and asked, "Do you want to hear a joke?" I thought I was ready. Nope, you're not going to catch me.

With the hubris of a marginally experienced teacher, I replied, "Would you tell this joke to your father or to your mother?" Smart, I thought. Now I was safe.

"It was my dad who told this joke to me last night," she replied sincerely. Hmmmm. Safe to proceed I thought.

"OK, go ahead and tell me."

This little girl then proceeded to tell me a joke that seemed innocent enough as she was telling it . . . until she got to the punch line.

This joke is one of the most sexually explicit jokes I have ever heard in my life—and that didn't become apparent until the very last line. I blushed, muttered something I cannot remember, and walked away embarrassed beyond words.

There is a very important lesson in this story for all of us who teach. Whenever a student asks you, "Do you want to hear a joke?" you will want to simply reply, "No, thanks—I'm too busy right now!" and walk away quickly. Or you may say, "No, thanks—my one and only friend tells me that I have no sense of humor."

Politely declining and walking away is likely the safest and the smartest thing you can do. You just cannot predict the punch line, and the punch line can be very embarrassing.

70. HOW TO USE MUSIC TO SOOTH A SAVAGE BEAST

"Music has charms to sooth a savage beast" is a common saying, and it has some interesting possibilities for teachers in classrooms.

It is likely that since the broadcast of the first radio waves, students the world over have wanted teachers to allow them to listen to music as they worked in their classrooms. And while many students will argue that listening to music helps them learn, likely just as many teachers remain suspect of this claim.

In their 2015 study, Ferreri, Bigand, and Bugaiska found that when students were exposed to *background instrumental music*, their ability to store new learnings in memory improved. Perhaps students are on to something.

While studies like this suggest that listening to music can be helpful, they are very specific as to the kind of music. . . *instrumental, soft, calming, pleasant to the ear*. Pachelbel's Canon and Bach's "Air on the G String" are good examples of this kind of music.

Given this, what role can music play in our classrooms? How can we use music to improve classroom behaviors and increase learning?

We all know—simply from personal experience and observation—that music can have a tremendous impact on our mood, on how we feel. Play Beethoven's *Sonata Pathetique*, Eric Clapton's "Tears in Heaven," or Labrinth's "Jealous" in your classroom and watch the room go quiet.

On the other hand, play "Wake Me Up before You Go-Go" (aka the Jitterbug song) by Wham! or Rick Astley's "Never Gonna Give You Up" or "Together Forever" and watch the energy in the room go way up.

You might be thinking, "This teacher is stuck in the 1980s. He's still listening to Wham! and Rick Astley in his classes." You would be wrong (see my current playlist at the end of this section).

For years, I have played these songs and others like them (bouncy, upbeat, full of energy—songs from many different decades) before the start of some of my classes in the mornings. As I write this section, I recall playing some 1980s music before the start of my class just last week as I sit here writing this, and I watched (once again, as I have many times before) the mood in the room change from very sleepy and low-key (this was an 8:00 a.m. class after all) to chatty, energy on the rise, and students smiling and interacting more.

People in the movie industry have used music to influence how they want the audience to feel since movies emerged out of the silent film era. There is something here for us as teachers.

You can influence the mood of your classrooms through music. This is another tool you can add to your *teacher toolbox*—and one that can be used to great effect.

And, if you're not sure what music your students find calming or upbeat, simply ask them for some recommendations. Knowing that you are going to play "their music" in class will most certainly get their attention.

If you want students to be working quietly, then play some soft instrumental background music. If you find their energy is low, play something bouncy and upbeat prior to class.

However you choose to use it, music can be an extremely effective tool that you can use to help your students achieve the learning goals that you set out for them.

Used wisely and used well, music can be a powerful addition to your teaching repertoire.

Note: The phrase "Music has charms to sooth a savage beast" originates from a poem entitled "The Mourning Bride," written by William Congreve in 1697. The original line of the poem states, "Musick has charms to soothe a savage breast," but over the years "breast" has been often misquoted as "beast."

By the way #1: Following is the twenty-three-song playlist that I currently use in my classroom. You will see that some are new; some are old; some are well known, while others are more obscure. I do not include this listing as any kind of scientific proof that these songs will work in your classroom; I just know that they work in mine.

By the way, as a little experiment, play any two or three of these songs in a row to yourself, and then check to see if your feet are tapping or your body is moving to the beat. Did your energy level go up a bit? How is your mood now?

- Keep the Car Running—Arcade Fire
- Livin' on a Prayer—Bon Jovi
- Born this Way—Lady Gaga
- Carry On—Fun
- Tub Thumping (I Get Knocked Down)—Chumba Wamba
- Heaven Is a Place on Earth—Belinda Carlisle
- I Don't Want to Go Home—Southside Johnny and the Asbury Jukes
- Don't Stop Believin'—Journey
- Hot N Cold—Katy Perry
- Waking Up in Vegas—Katy Perry
- Brandy—Looking Glass
- Don't Stop Me Now—Queen
- Never Going to Give You Up—Rick Astley
- Together Forever—Rick Astley
- Disturbia—Rihanna
- Run Runaway—Slade
- That Thing You Do—The Wonders
- I Gotta Feeling—The Black Eyed Peas
- Waka Waka (This Time for Africa)—Shakira
- Wake Me Up before You Go-Go—Wham
- You're So Beautiful—Jussie Smollett and Yazz
- Bang Bang—Ariana Grande, Jessie J, and Nicki Minaj

By the way #2: There is another strategy you can use to change the mood in your classroom if you believe the mood needs changing. Go to YouTube and search for "babies laughing" or perhaps "babies dancing" and show this to your class. It is virtually impossible to look at some of these "babies laughing compilations" and not start laughing yourself. Your students will too.

71. WHEN YOU'RE SICK, TIRED, CRANKY, OR HAVING A BAD DAY

All of us have bad days. Even the healthiest teacher gets sick on occasion. Even the happiest among us feels down at times.

The question for you as a teacher then becomes: What do you do when this happens to you? What do you do if you are not feeling well, but still choose to go to school? How do you handle your classes when you are feeling really down (perhaps due to strains in a relationship or the death of someone close) and you find yourself starting the school day and you just can't shake the feeling?

Some teachers try the "fake it till they make it" strategy. They attempt to put on a false front and pretend that things are normal.

Generally it is often easier to fool adults than it is to fool kids. Kids seem to have this strong intuitive sense, and if you choose to fake it, your students will likely pick up on the fact that you are "off" and that things feel different on days such as these.

Rather than attempting to fake it, you should instead consider being completely honest with your students. If you are sick, injured, overtired, or struggling in any way with other aspects of life, simply tell your students that you are not your normal self and that you need them to understand that the class might not run as it usually does today. Let them know that you might not be quite as patient or upbeat and energetic as is normal for you.

When you do this, most often, the best in your students comes out. This is especially true if you have already established a good relationship with the kids in your class.

If they know you are not well, if they know that your grandmother just passed away and you are really sad, you will likely see them at their most compassionate. They will likely be supportive and kind, and you will be proud of them (and perhaps you may even feel just a little bit better because of them).

Having said that, you still need to be careful about how much of your personal life you share with your students. It is one thing to tell your students that you are feeling low because your grandmother died. It is entirely another thing to tell them that your relationship is falling apart because your partner cheated on you.

There are lines that should not be crossed, and common sense will most often show you where they are. If in doubt, check with a mentor teacher or your administrator.

72. YOU ARE RARELY THE TARGET—EVEN WHEN THEY'RE AIMING AT YOU

There are times when students simply "lose it" while at school. They will display an emotional outburst over which they have little or no control whatsoever. With younger children, this kind of outburst will often manifest itself in uncontrollable crying and/or screaming.

At other times, more typically with older students, these eruptions may take the form of yelling and swearing—sometimes aimed directly at you. You may hear a student call you every vile name in the English language—and then add a few words you have never heard of before. They may well be kicking walls, throwing chairs, and slamming doors as they do this.

Sometimes, older students—out of anger, frustration, or simply in an attempt to gain some status with their peers—will confront you in a very disrespectful way in front of the entire class.

While it is difficult not to take these types of behaviors personally, please try to remember—*this is not about you!*

Brain research informs us that in young children and teenagers, the frontal cortex (the site of judgment and problem solving) develops at a *significantly slower rate* than the limbic part of the brain (the site of emotions and stimulation).

This helps explain why teenagers tend to take unnecessary risks and why they can often be extremely reactive in situations without considering future consequences of their actions. This is the limbic brain overriding the frontal cortex.

As well, try to remember that your students—just like you—have lives outside of school. They too bring their outside lives to class with them every day. Sometimes they are struggling with issues and burdens that are far

Figure 4.5.

beyond their capacity to carry gracefully, and the weight of these can get to them some days.

So, if a student ever loses it on you or confronts you in class, try to stay calm and let them "get it all out" if this course of action is feasible.

It is very unlikely that the explosion you are witnessing has much—if anything at all—to do directly with you. Rather, it is most likely a result of things in the student's life that have nothing whatsoever to do with you, and the limbic brain is in full display in all its ignominious glory.

Remember: you are not the target. You just happen to be in the line of fire. You're simply collateral damage in situations such as this.

By the way: There is an ancient parable from India (adapted as follows from *The Parables of Ramakrishna: The Snake That Refused to Hiss*) that has a great deal of wisdom for us as teachers when we are dealing with students who are behaving in unacceptable ways. It goes like this:

Some cowherd boys used to tend their cows in a meadow where a terrible poisonous snake lived. All the boys were constantly on the alert for fear of the snake. One day a wise man was walking along the meadow. The boys ran to him and said, "Sir, please don't go that way. A poisonous snake lives over there."

"What of it, my good children?" said the wise man. "I am not afraid of the snake." So saying, he continued on his way.

A short time later, the snake saw the man and moved swiftly toward him, ready to strike.

As soon as the snake came near, the man asked kindly, "Look here. Why do you go about doing harm? Come, I will give you a holy word. By repeating it you will learn to love God. Ultimately you will realize Him and so get rid of your violent nature."

Saying this, he taught the snake a holy word. The snake bowed before the teacher and said, "Revered sir, how will I practice spiritual discipline?"

"Repeat that sacred word," said the teacher, "and do no harm to anybody." As he was about to depart, the old man said, "I shall see you again."

Some days passed, and the cowherd boys noticed that the snake would no longer bite. They threw stones at it. Still it showed no anger. One day one of the boys came close to it, caught it by the tail, and whirling it round and round, dashed it again and again on the ground and then threw it away. The snake vomited blood and became unconscious. It was stunned. It could not move. So, thinking it dead, the boys went their way.

Later that night, the snake regained consciousness. Slowly and with great difficulty, it dragged itself into its hole; its bones were broken, and it could scarcely move. The snake became a mere skeleton covered with a skin. It maintained its life on dirt, leaves, or the fruit that dropped from the trees.

About a year later, the wise man came that way again and asked about the snake. The cowherd boys told him that it was dead since they had not seen it for a very long time. But the old man didn't believe them. He went to the place where he first met the snake and called it by the name he had given it. Hearing the teacher's voice, the snake came out of its hole and bowed before him with great reverence.

"How are you?" asked the old man.

"I am well, sir," replied the snake.

"But why are you so thin?" the wise man asked.

The snake replied, "Sir, you ordered me not to harm anybody. So I have been living only on leaves and fruit. Perhaps that has made me thinner."

The old man said: "It can't be mere want of food that has reduced you to this state. There must be some other reason. Think a little."

Then the snake answered, "Now I remember. One day one of the boys dashed me violently against the ground. They are ignorant, after all. They didn't realize what a great change had come over my mind. How could they know I wouldn't bite or harm anyone?"

The old man exclaimed: "What a shame! You are such a fool! You don't know how to protect yourself. I asked you not to bite, but I didn't forbid you to hiss. Why didn't you scare them by hissing?"

Please remember: *sometimes, when you are dealing with students who have stepped over the line, you have to hiss!*

73. EVERY ARTIST WAS FIRST AN AMATEUR

Ralph Waldo Emerson said, "Every artist was first an amateur." There is a great lesson here for teachers. *Be patient with yourself!*

You cannot become a master teacher in your first year, or your second, or your third . . . You may be a great beginning teacher, but it is not possible to be a truly great teacher in your first few years of teaching.

Why is that?

By the time you have reached this part of this book, you should have a good sense of how complex teaching really is. Teaching is "people work"—and people are complicated and ever-changing.

Trying to determine the best way to teach particular concepts to a particular group of kids is challenging, and in order to do this well, you need two things. First, you need to know the kids really well. Second, you need to have a wide range of teaching techniques and strategies on hand to be able to draw from.

The "toolbox" analogy works well to describe how important it is for a teacher to develop a wide repertoire of teaching techniques and strategies.

For example, if a person only has a hammer, a saw, and a measuring tape in their toolbox—only three tools—they will be able to build some things and repair some other things, but not very much. They won't be able to work with bolts or screws, they can't cut metal, and they can't grip items with pliers or strip electrical wire. They don't have the necessary tools.

If you want to become a great teacher, you must continually add to your "teaching toolbox." You must become intimately familiar with the *curriculum*; you must learn and become adept at using a wide *variety of teaching strategies*; you must become familiar with various *assessment tools*; you must know and gain access to a wide range of curricularly appropriate *teaching resources*; you will need to develop *effective working relationships with your students*; and you will need to have a very refined sense of *what is happening in your classroom at all times.*

All this takes time to develop and learn—a great deal of time.

This last tool—an acute awareness of what is happening in your classroom—is especially helpful in preventing class management and discipline problems.

In sports, it is often said that *some superstars see the game in slow motion.* They have a sense of what *is* happening—and what is *going to* happen—that few people ever develop. A few years ago, a very famous hockey player, talking about Wayne Gretsky, made the statement that he never saw the game the way Gretsky did.

The same can be said of "superstar" teachers. They "see the classroom" in ways other teachers do not.

You can see seasoned teachers who are talking to the class as a whole from the front of the room, then they deliberately move from the front of the room in order to stand close to a particular student or group of students in a different part of the classroom.

When asked why this relocation, they will often reply, "I sensed something was up."

When asked what were the clues that the kids were off topic or distracted or at the beginning stages of getting into mischief, frequently these veteran teachers simply can't give a specific answer. Their reply is often, "I don't know how I knew. *I just knew.*"

It takes a lot of years to develop that kind of classroom awareness. This is what Malcolm Gladwell writes about in *Blink* when he says, "From experience, we gain a powerful gift, the ability to act instinctively, in the moment." You simply cannot have that gift without first acquiring a great deal of experience—and acquiring experience takes time, a great deal of time.

If, year after year, you diligently add more tools to your teaching toolbox, you will find that over time you have many different tools to draw upon in your teaching, your class management, your discipline strategies, and your assessments. Because of this, you are more likely to both *have the proper tools* and *to use these tools appropriately* in order to be successful in your teaching.

So please, be patient with yourself. No one has ever become a master teacher overnight, or even in a year or two. It takes time, and practice, and time, and reflection, and experience, and time.

It takes many years to move from amateur to artist—in athletics, painting, in acting, in music. Teaching is no exception.

74. YOU ARE NEVER DONE

In #66, you were encouraged to be patient with your students when they struggle to learn or misbehave because *they're not done yet.*

Well, the same applies to you and your growth as a teacher: *you're not done yet either!*

All great teachers have a tremendous work ethic, and fundamental to this work ethic is *an ethic of continuous improvement.* Great teachers are constantly trying to become better at teaching, they are continually learning: learning about the subjects they teach, the students they teach, how kids learn, and they work hard to absorb anything else they think will assist them in helping their students to learn.

Great teachers are naturally curious and are constantly learning themselves.

Much of what great teachers learn about teaching is taught to them by their students.

Great teachers realize they simply don't know everything and will never know everything. They are not afraid to be vulnerable in front of their students and say, "I don't know the answer to that—but let's find out!"

As well, they are not the least bit afraid of having students teach them—sometimes about course content, and other times about "what is going to work well in this classroom with this group of kids."

If you want to be a great teacher, you are going to need an *ethic of continuous improvement* due to the very nature of the teaching profession. What is meant by this?

If you teach for a long time, you will most certainly experience a great deal of change:

- First, the kids change every year—every fall, a whole new batch.
- Second, you may change grades and/or schools, and with changes like these comes a whole new curriculum to learn or a new school culture to learn.
- Third, the curriculum will change. Old resources fall out of use, and new ones are adopted. As well, governments rewrite curriculum from time to time, and when they do, you find yourself teaching a new curriculum. Once again, you are in some ways a first-year teacher.
- Fourth, educational technology changes. Teachers have gone from blackboards to whiteboards to smartboards. You can be certain that technologies such as virtual reality, augmented reality, and artificial intelligence will find their way into classrooms more and more as time goes on.

You will see many changes in the "tools of the trade" in teaching, and you will have to master how to use them—and then determine how to "best" use them and when to use them to maximum effect in your classroom.

Be happy with things when they go well in your classroom. Be pleased with yourself and your students when you see progress being made and real learning taking place. But at the same time, realize that *you can always improve on everything you do in teaching*.

You are never done!

By the way: There is a saying that you may find to be extremely helpful in assisting you in finding the right balance between being happy with what you are achieving with your students, yet at the same time realizing that you can still do things better. It is a saying that you have read previously in this book, one good teachers take to heart. *Progress, not perfection!*

Perfectionists ultimately perish, because perfection is impossible to attain. You should strive for *progress, not perfection*—continually try to get better, and at the same time, realize that nothing you do will ever be perfect, and that's alright.

75. WHEN YOU STOP LEARNING, YOU ARE DONE

In #74, we explored the idea that as a teacher, "You are never done." Nonetheless, there are, sadly, teachers who are an exception to this.

There is the story told of the teacher who, at the end of his first year, laminated his plan book. This teacher stayed at the same school and taught the same grade for two decades. Twenty years later, he bragged that he had taught for twenty years. But the truth is, he has *not* taught for twenty years. Rather, he has taught *one year twenty times*.

The exception to the "you are never done" statement are the teachers who—due to laziness or hubris—think they have mastered all they need to know about teaching, and they stop learning.

They stop learning about their kids, and instead they teach every class as if this group of students was just like all of the other groups of students they have taught. They make no allowance for individual or group difference— even though these differences are always there.

They stop learning about the curriculum, because as long as the curriculum stays the same, they continue to use the same resources and use these resources in the same ways—the ways they are familiar with. They don't seek out more interesting or relevant materials that would better engage their students. No need, they believe—and far too much work.

They stop learning about educational technology. "The old ways are the best ways," they say as they clean their acetate transparency rolls on the overhead projector. Best for whom—them or their students?

These kinds of teachers have failed to make a serious commitment to life-long learning. These kinds of teachers have failed to learn from their students, to learn from their colleagues, and to learn from reading and courses and life.

Your students will hope that you never become this kind of teacher, and so should you.

76. YOU DON'T BRING IN AN ELEPHANT TO TEACH THE COLOR GRAY

A presenter at an in-service program on how to be a better teacher made this statement, "You don't bring in an elephant to teach the color gray!" She then repeated this (she was a good teacher—she used repetition effectively), "You don't bring in an elephant to teach the color gray!"

She went on to explain that if you were a kindergarten teacher and you were attempting to teach the color gray to your students, one strategy you could use to accomplish this would be to bring a baby elephant into the classroom. It would be an experience that the kids would be unlikely to ever forget.

However, there is a problem with this strategy.

The problem is this: in selecting resources, teaching materials, and experiences—the materials you use to teach the ideas and knowledge you want your students to learn—*how can you best ensure that these resources and experiences support and enhance what you want your students to learn, rather than becoming the object of learning in themselves?*

This is a very challenging question.

For example, you can have early elementary students throwing koosh balls at colored circles on a smartboard to help them identify and learn their colors ("Hit the color red now"), but is that an effective way to teach color recognition? Will the kids remember the colors, or will they get so engaged in throwing the koosh balls that in fact the method of teaching these concepts becomes an *obstacle* rather than an *aid* to helping the students learn colors?

Ideally, as a teacher, you want to structure experiences and use resources that support the achievement of your learning objectives—not experiences and resources that get in the way—no matter how "cool" these activities are.

So remember, "You don't bring in an elephant to teach the color gray."

By the way: Curriculum design and lesson planning are very tricky. There are so many variables to consider—not the least of which is the group of students you are teaching (and these students change constantly—not just from year to year, but from day to day). What are they interested in? What metaphors, analogies, examples, and illustrations would work best for *this group* of kids? You will never get it just right, and that's OK. Remember, you are aiming for *progress, not perfection!*

77. HOW DO YOU EAT AN ELEPHANT?

There is an old saying that says: "How do you eat an elephant—one bite at a time." There is much wisdom in this for teachers.

Often, teachers try to give far too much content to students, far too soon. Under pressure to "cover the curriculum" and feeling there is never enough time, it is tempting for teachers to go through course content quickly, with little to no depth or without checking for student understanding before moving on.

This is what the high school social studies teacher in #51 did—he covered content quickly, far too quickly. And while he probably taught the entire course content, there was, however, little learning by his students. He argued that he "taught it," but many of his students didn't learn it.

As we plan our school year and look at the curriculum we are supposed to teach, it can indeed appear to be the size of an elephant—there is simply so much to teach and so little time. It can be very tempting for us as educators to rush through content so that we feel good because "we covered it all."

We may have "covered it," but can we honestly say we have "taught it" if our students haven't "learned it?"

As teachers, we need to give our students learning in bite-size chunks, the size our students can take in, understand, and digest. If we try and force-feed too much content or content that is beyond what our students are ready for, there will not be much—if any—learning going on.

In light of this, think about this question: *Why don't we teach calculus to Grade 6 students?* We don't do this because we know two things.

First, the typical Grade 6 child's brain is not developed enough to understand the abstract concepts necessary to comprehend calculus.

Second, we know that in order to understand calculus, you need to have several other layers of mathematical understanding in place first. Without a good understanding of algebra and trigonometry, you simply cannot do calculus. And, in order to understand algebra, you need to understand symbolic math. In order to understand trigonometry, you need to understand geometry and shapes and their formulas and structures.

For the same reason, we don't teach *Hamlet* in Grade 3. The students do not yet have the requisite skills in English to tackle literary works of such complexity.

In teaching, we call this *scaffolding*—the building of more advanced knowledge upon the foundations and layers of previous knowledge.

As so, at the beginning of the school year, when you look at "the elephant" that is the curriculum for the entire year, please don't try and force-feed it to your students in big, indigestible chunks.

Rather, learn what your students already know relative to curricular knowledge and skills, and start building from there.

You must *meet your students where they're at!* There really is no other effective place to start.

78. WHY WE DON'T TRY TO TEACH A PIG TO FLY

There is a common saying that goes, "Don't try to teach a pig to fly. It will only frustrate you, and it annoys the pig."

This can also be said another way: "No matter how long you build the runway, pigs still can't fly."

Figure 4.6.

There is a great truth here for us as teachers, and it is that we need to always remember that *all students have limits*, and some students are more limited in their abilities than others.

For example, let's say you are trying to teach a particular concept to a group of students, such as globalization in social studies or anthropomorphism in an English class. You teach these concepts, and then you give the students some guided practice and check if they understand what you have just taught. You then discover there are three students who clearly don't understand these concepts at all.

So, you work with these three students. You try to teach these concepts one way, then a different way. Eventually, two of these students show a basic understanding of the terms, but the third student still doesn't get it. You try and try again. Still, understanding is not there.

If you know this student well, you might reach a valid conclusion that no matter how hard you try, and no matter how hard the student tries, this student is not going to understand these concepts. Why? Not because he or she is lazy, not because he or she is not trying, and not because you are a poor teacher.

The honest answer may simply be that these concepts are *too far above his or her intellectual abilities*. Even if the student gives it all he or she has got, he or she may still not understand what you are trying to teach.

It is difficult for us as teachers to realize that sometimes—the content that is so familiar to us, so easy for us, and so obvious to us is so challenging for our students.

To continue trying to push a student well beyond his or her abilities in a situation such as this will frustrate both the student *and* the teacher. It would be akin to a basketball coach trying to teach a five-foot-tall Grade 6 student how to slam-dunk a basketball. It's just not going to happen no matter how hard the student tries.

In cases like this, it is time to move on. Don't frustrate your students, and don't be annoyed at yourself, and don't try and build a longer runway. Just move on.

By the way: When you run into a situation such as the one described here, there is a strategy you can use that will most likely help the student feel better. If you see the student really trying hard and still can't grasp the concept after repeated attempts, you will often hear students in situations such as this say, "I can't do this!"

You can respond with, "That's true, you can't do this—*today*. We will try again tomorrow, and maybe then you will understand this, and if you don't, we will try the day after that. You will eventually understand this, just not today, and that's OK. We will try again tomorrow."

Give the students the confidence to believe in themselves, to k
eventually they will learn the material, and that it's OK if they don't understand it today. After all, you both have tomorrow.

79. THE IKEA EFFECT: THE PRIDE WE FEEL IN WORK WE DO OURSELVES

In his book *Payoff: The Hidden Logic That Shapes Our Motivations*, Dan
Ariely (2016) discusses what he calls the IKEA effect. He describes how dif-
ficult and frustrating it can be trying to follow the directions that come with
IKEA furniture in our attempts to put their furniture together.

And yet, he noticed that of all the furniture in his home, it is the IKEA
furniture—*the furniture that he assembled himself*—that gave him the greatest sense of satisfaction and accomplishment.

This pride of accomplishment in work we do ourselves (even when the
work is challenging or frustrating) was noticed back in the 1940s by a cake
mix company by the name of P. Duff and Sons. When they introduced cake
mixes in a box—where housewives only had to add water, stir and bake—the
cakes tasted good, but did not sell well. Duff discovered that the housewives
of that era felt that just adding water to a mix and then baking did not feel to
them like they had made the cake themselves.

So Duff took out the powdered eggs and powdered milk from the mix,
forcing the housewives to add eggs and milk on their own. The new cake
mixes—although requiring more ingredients and more work—sold very well.
Why? Housewives reported that they now felt that they had baked the cake
themselves, and thus they were much happier with the end product. It was
their cake. They had made it.

What is the lesson here for us as teachers?

Both of these examples show us *the incredible power of effort and ownership.* When we work hard, when we overcome obstacles and work through
frustrations, when the creation at the end of our efforts (be it a piece of furniture, a cake, or a lesson—unit plan) comes together, it is ours. We created it,
we own it, and we get joy and satisfaction from the fruits of our labor.

That is why the lesson plans that *we construct* for our students; the unit
plans that *we make* for our students; the activities *we plan* for our students,
and the assessments *we create* for our students—these most often feel like
they are *better* than resources we can get online or from colleagues.

As teachers, we have a lot of demands on our time, and limited time to
meet those demands. Thus, we will often find that we need to use resources
created by others. That is both appropriate and necessary.

But *how* we use those resources, how we *customize* the way we use other people's work in our classrooms, is critical. It is critical to our feeling of ownership, and it is critical to how successful our students will be in their learning.

It is a great truth in teaching that the very best lesson plans most teachers ever see . . . are the ones they make themselves. Why? *Because they made them; because they made them for their students.*

When we use materials in our classrooms that we have created, or that we have adapted to better suit the needs of our students, we feel a sense of connection with the materials, a sense of ownership, and our sense of identity as a teacher is more closely linked to the success of these materials in our classrooms.

Never underestimate the power of ownership and effort in your lesson planning—aka the IKEA effect. *By the way:* I mentioned earlier in this book that I have taught close to 40,000 lessons throughout my career—and none of them, *not one of them*, went exactly according to my lesson plan. Why is that, you might ask? Poor planning? Poor execution? *No!*

None of my lesson plans went exactly according to plan because of. . . *students*! When you walk into your classroom with a lesson plan, that classroom will be filled with students. These students will have questions; they will have moods; some will engage in the material and some will not; some will be upset at things happening outside of the classroom, while others will be calm. When planning your lessons, you cannot know any of these variables, because they vary from class to class, day to day, and even from minute to minute within each class. Thus, you must learn to *improvise*.

Years ago, the effective teaching movement labeled this "monitor and adjust." Same idea. Because classrooms are very unpredictable places, you must learn to *think on your feet*, be *flexible* with your lesson plan, and *adjust* to what is happening in your classroom—minute by minute. Again we are reminded, "Darling, you must learn to adjust!"

Be patient with yourself in this regard. This takes a lot of time and experience. You can get there—with a lot of looking, a lot of listening, and lot of patience, and a lot of practice.

80. IF YOU ARE WORKING HARDER THAN YOUR STUDENTS IN CLASS, YOU'RE DOING IT WRONG!

Oftentimes in education, you will see the following chart or pyramid about how people learn. It states that we learn:

- 10 percent of what we *read*
- 20 percent of what we *hear*

- 30 percent of what we *see*
- 70 percent of what is *discussed with others*
- 80 percent of what we *experience* personally
- 90 percent of what we *teach*

There are a lot of problems with this chart—its dubious origins and its percentage specificity. However, in a general sense, there is a worthwhile message here for teachers.

Clearly, this chart and our personal experiences tell us that we forget a great deal of what we read and hear, but we tend to remember more readily personal experiences and materials that we have had to learn in order to teach.

How can this help us as teachers? Simple! The message is: *If you are doing more work in your classroom than your students, you are doing it wrong!*

This does not refer to more work *overall* (such as your lesson preparation, resource gathering, marking, and the like). What this refers to is what is going on in the classroom *while you are actually teaching.*

If you are doing most of the work and the kids are just sitting there, it is highly probable that they are fading in and out of attentiveness to what you are saying. It is unlikely that there is much learning going on.

In order for students to maximize their learning, they need to be *actively engaged in the learning work,* and sitting and listening for long periods of time does not qualify as active engagement.

Your first task lies in the preparation. You need to prepare lessons and assessments and projects that are curricularly focused, relevant to the students, achievable, and engaging. These need to challenge the students and make them get involved—involved in solving a mystery, exploring possible answers to big questions, and the like.

Once this is accomplished, your task is to *get them working during class time at the work you have prepared for them*—working with the materials and experiences and assessments that you have planned, while you observe and guide them through this work.

This is why in the classrooms of master teachers, you will often see the teacher working with a small group of students or with a student individually, or simply standing against the wall observing, and only moving in to talk to students when he or she senses the need. These teachers have already done their work at the beginning of the class when they introduced the lesson and set the stage for learning. Now it is time for the students to do their work.

Remember, some of *your* most important work occurs *outside* of the classroom, gathering resources, structuring engaging learning experiences, planning how to assess student learning, and so forth.

Inside the classroom, for the most part, *you will want to let your students get to work.*

81. THE VIRTUE OF FRUSTRATION

Most teachers are, by nature, helpful. We went into this profession because we like to help people. It makes us feel good; it gives us a sense of accomplishment and a sense of purpose.

However, sometimes teachers can be too quick to be helpful, and there is a danger in this for our students.

If we "ride to the rescue" too quickly each time a student asks for our help, there is a danger that we are creating a form of dependence.

While there are certainly times when a teacher should help a student in difficulty, there are other times when *we do our students a superior service by letting them struggle and try and figure things out for themselves.*

This can build resolve, perseverance, and determination; it can build confidence; and it certainly builds independence. Sometimes it is a better choice to *let your students be frustrated and keep searching for solutions on their own.*

How do we know when to help students and when instead we should send them on their way to continue to work on the problem by themselves or to seek help elsewhere?

That's a tough call.

You have to get to a point where you can "read the student"—where you develop a sense of when to help and when to step away.

Good teachers want to move their students toward ever-increasing levels of independence and self-sufficiency. You would be a very poor teacher indeed if your students were as dependent on you at the end of the year as they were at the beginning.

If you choose to let the students struggle further on their own, you do need to turn them away kindly and supportively.

A response such as "I can see you're frustrated, but I have confidence in you. I know you can solve this on your own without me. Let me know when you do" can send a student away with a bit more confidence and determination.

Don't be too quick to help or rescue your students all of the time. Read the signs, then proceed accordingly.

By the way: It is unfortunate, but you will find some students—too many students—who will be paralyzed by their *fear of failure*. Somewhere along their life's journey, they were taught that failing was unacceptable, that it made them unworthy in some ways. This is often exemplified by the parent/caregiver who, when their child brings home a mark of let's say 96 percent on a test, asks, "Which ones did you get wrong?"

There is a story told that Thomas Edison was being interviewed by a reporter shortly after he had invented the light bulb. The reporter asked

Edison how many attempts it took him to invent the light bulb. Edison replied that he had conducted about 1,000 experiments before things finally worked. The reporter then asked Edison, "How did it feel to fail 1,000 times?" Edison replied, "I didn't fail 1,000 times. The light bulb was invented in 1,000 steps!"

This is similar to the story behind the development of WD40. The WD40 company website credits the invention of WD40 to one Norman Larsen, founder of the Rocket Chemical Company. Larsen was attempting to create a water displacement chemical and allegedly took forty attempts to get it just right . . . hence the name: "WD40."

The lesson here is clear. Very few of us—whether we are students or whether we are teachers—get things right the first time we try. We all need to recognize and accept that we are going to fail from time to time; we are going to get frustrated; and we are going to have to keep trying over and over again until we get it right—maybe forty times; maybe 1,000 times. You need to remind your students of this—and perhaps yourself as well.

As a teacher, you should eliminate the word "failure" from your classroom. Replace it with "learning experience"—as in, "You didn't fail—you had a learning experience. Now, use that to do better the next time."

82. LET THIS YEAR'S STUDENTS HELP MAKE YOUR COURSES BETTER FOR NEXT YEAR

One of the differences between you and your students is that while of you may both be in the same room for the same lessons; you will certainly *not* have the same experiences as your students do. You will not experience life in your classroom the same way as your students do, and you will certainly not experience the courses you teach in the same way as they do.

That is why it is crucial that you obtain feedback from your students about *their experiences* in order to determine how successful you have been in helping them to learn—and equally important, how you can improve your teaching and your courses for your students in the future.

At the end of each year (yes, even in elementary school), it is an excellent idea to have students do a course review sheet for you. Simply tell them that you need this information in order to make the course better for the kids who will be in your class next year, and that the kids you taught the year before had made the course better for them by providing you with this invaluable information.

This is not a complex task, and it does not take a great deal of time. However, the information you obtain through this feedback can prove to be insightful and valuable to you in making improvements to your course content and delivery in subsequent years.

Simply have your students answer these five questions, and have them respond in writing anonymously:

1. Which topic(s) or units(s) had the most impact on you? Why?
2. What did you like *best* about this course? Please explain.
3. What did you like *least* about this course? Please explain.
4. Of all the things we did this term, what are the *three things* you think you will remember for the rest of your life? Why these three?
5. General comments and suggestions for making this course better for next year?

Pay close attention to their answers. *They know things you don't.*

83. SO YOU REACHED THE END OF JUNE— TIME TO LOOK BACK

Congratulations! You made it—the end of a school year.

It is tempting near the end of the school year to focus on the upcoming summer holidays and such things as plans with friends and family to relax and to therefore *not* think about school and curriculum and kids, and understandably so.

Having said this, however, the end of the school year is an opportune time for you to spend some time reflecting on the school year that has just past. Events are still relatively fresh in your mind, and if you take a bit of time to do some reflecting on the year that just past, you have the opportunity to take those lessons forward and make your next school year even better.

Following are some questions to get you started. These are the kinds of questions that are extremely important for any teacher to ponder—whether you're ending your first year of teaching or your thirty-first year of teaching.

1. What have you taught successfully this past year?

    a. Did you teach the prescribed curriculum? Did you take your students through all or most of the content they need to be successful next year? Are you confident that your students are ready for the next school year in terms of the knowledge, skills, and values they will need because of what you did in your courses this year?

    b. Did you teach by example? Did you show your students—by the example that you lived in your classroom—that the things you said were important (honesty, hard work, punctuality, kindness, forgiveness, compassion, etc.) were really important, so important that you modeled them every day?

c. Did you show your students that they were important, that you truly cared for them—both as students and as people—that they had value and worth beyond what they scored on tests and assignments?

d. Did you learn enough about your students as individuals that you were able to successfully know how to motivate, encourage, and support each of them in the ways they needed?

2. *What did you do exceptionally well this past year?*

a. What were your three biggest highlights—the three things that you did that were successful and meaningful well beyond what you ever thought possible?

b. Who were the students that you did exceptionally well with this past year? These are the students who may have appeared to be the most difficult and challenging at the beginning of the year, but by the end of the year you had established a great relationship with and now they were working to potential.

3. *What did you learn this past year?*

a. What were your most significant learnings in regard to how to *teach* kids at this age level?

b. What were your most significant learnings in regard to how to *motivate* kids at this age level?

c. What were your most significant learnings in regard to how to *establish effective working relationships* with kids at this age level?

d. What were your most significant learnings in regard to how to *assess* kids at this age level?

e. What were your *biggest surprises* in regard to working with kids at this age level?

4. *What do you need to work on next year?*

a. What would you say were your *most significant mistakes in terms of teaching* this year? What do you need to do to improve on these for next year?

b. What would you say were your *most significant mistakes in terms of your relationships with your students* this year? What do you need to do to improve on these for next year?

c. What would you say were your *most significant mistakes in terms of your relationships with your students' parents/caregivers* this year? What do you need to do to improve on these for next year?

    d. What would you say were your *most significant mistakes in terms of your relationships with your colleagues* this year? What do you need to do to improve on these for next year?

Please do not "beat yourself up" at the end of the school year as you go over your responses to these questions. No teacher ever had a perfect school year. We all slip and fall. The point of these reflections is for you to take what you discover here and to use the information to improve your teaching and the classroom experiences of your students in the following school year.

By the way: If you want to get your students' perspective on how to make things better in your classroom, every once in a while throughout the year, you can ask them to answer to this question: "If I were the teacher I would _____ to improve our classroom."

This can be done individually where the students hand in a written response, or it can be done in groups where students discuss it with one another and then a spokesperson for the group reports their conclusions to you and the class verbally.

This is a strategy that can be used throughout the year on occasion and not simply reserved for the end of the year so you have ideas to improve things going into the next school year.

This gives students a sense of ownership and a degree of control over their class, and you will get some great suggestions—suggestions that come from the students' perspective—sometimes ideas you would likely never think of yourself.

Section Five

What You Need to Do during the Second and Third Years of Teaching, and Going Forward from There

What do you need to work on during your second and third years of teaching and beyond? If you are doing things well, the answer to that question is really very simple—*more of the same, just better!*

After teaching for a year, all teachers with any degree of self-awareness know that they still have a lot to work on. Some things will have gone well; other things will have even gone exceptionally well. Still, at other times, you will have faced situations that you never expected, and you now recognize that you handled them poorly.

In other cases, you will have dealt with people and circumstances in ways that you thought at the time were effective and appropriate—because the tools you used then were all you had available to you.

Now, with more experience and more awareness to draw upon, you recognize that there are better ways to deal with certain circumstances—better way to teach, better ways to deal with students in particular situations, better ways to work with parents/caregivers—and now you are going to try to do some things in ways that you believe will be more effective.

You have read all eighty-three ideas, and you may have attempted to implement many of them. However, looking back, you may see that some of these ideas just don't work for you and your students, or they don't fit your personality or your style of teaching.

Perhaps you tried to implement some of these eighty-three strategies, but now recognize that you did not do so very effectively, so in your next year of teaching you are going to give these strategies another try—only this time in a different way and hopefully with greater effectiveness.

This will most certainly result in your students benefiting from your work at becoming a better teacher. This is reflective teaching in action. This is lifelong learning. This is an ethic of continuous improvement. And most importantly, this is you working your way toward becoming a master teacher.

Ang Lee, the director of such well-known films as *Crouching Tiger, Hidden Dragon*; *Brokeback Mountain*; and *The Life of Pi*, had been directing movies for over twenty years before he finally won the Academy Award for Best Director in 2013 for *The Life of Pi*.

It took Lee over twenty years to achieve this award, which acknowledged his outstanding abilities as a film director, yet he said, "I am still a novice student" in regard to his abilities to direct films. Twenty-plus years—and still learning! Lee also said of his directing career, "I did a women's movie, and I'm not a woman. I did a gay movie, and I'm not gay. I learned as I went along."

You are strongly encouraged to adopt the attitude Ang Lee has toward directing movies in your teaching. Take this posture: *I am still a novice—I am still learning* and *I will learn as I go along*.

In her book *Teacher as Stranger*, Maxine Greene (1973) encouraged teachers to constantly strive to see their students, their classrooms, their work as though looking at these things for the first time, as though looking at the students and the curriculum and the classroom environment *through the eyes of a stranger—as if they were constantly new*. The *Zeigarnik effect* demonstrates why this is so important for you as a teacher.

One evening in the early 1900s, psychologists Kurt Lewin and Bluma Zeigarnik were out for supper with a large group of friends, and they were amazed at how accurately their waiter took their order (without writing anything down) and how he then later delivered each different dinner flawlessly to the correct person after it had been prepared. As an experiment (after all, they couldn't resist; that is what psychologists do—they experiment), they then covered their plates with napkins and asked the waiter to tell them what order was under each napkin. The waiter couldn't do this.

At first, they were puzzled by the waiter's amazing memory, followed so shortly thereafter with an almost complete lack of recollection. After some deliberation and discussion, they thought they had figured out what was going on—and subsequent studies have proven them correct. What is now known as the *Zeigarnik effect* states that people will remember uncompleted tasks with greater accuracy than completed tasks. Once a task is completed, our mind automatically files this task under the "done" category, and shifts its focus onto what we need to accomplish next.

For the waiter, once an order had been taken accurately, then delivered to the table accurately, his mind moved on to what had to be dealt with next. There is a very profound lesson in this for us as teachers.

If you ever get to a point in your career where you think you are finished learning about teaching because you believe you have mastered the curriculum, you know all the teaching and assessment strategies you will ever need, and you are certain that you know the type of students you are teaching, then you will be a victim of the *Zeigarnik effect.* You think you have *finished* the work of becoming a teacher—that task is *done!*

If this happens, you will not attend to the students in front of you properly; you will not see them for who they truly are and what they need; and you will not engage them with curriculum in ways that are meaningful to them. Rather, you will be like the teacher who laminated their plan book after the first year of teaching and proceeded to teach the same things for the next twenty years.

Robert Cialdini describes the power of this effect in his 2016 book *Pre-suasion*, "on a task that we feel committed to performing, we will remember all sorts of elements of it better if we have not yet had the chance to finish, because our attention will remain drawn to it."

If you are going to remain attentive to your teaching skills and to your students, you must realize that your development as a teacher is never finished, because if you ever think you have mastered it all, your performance will most certainly diminish, and your students will lose out.

In a sense, if you think you're finished—you are!

In 2017, Walter Isaacson's book on the life of Leonardo da Vinci was published. This massive biography was based in large part on the over 7,200 pages of notes that da Vinci wrote and that the author had access to. Scribbled in these notes are drawings of birds, flying machines, moving water, blood flow through the body, angels, plants, skulls, notes on how the eye works along with ideas for weapons of war, and much more.

As well, there are numerous to-do lists, describing things that da Vinci wanted to learn each day, like observe a goose's foot and figure out how a woodpecker's skull can absorb so much impact.

Isaacson describes da Vinci's notebooks as "the greatest record of curiosity ever created, a wondrous guide to the person whom the eminent art historian Kenneth Clark called 'the most relentlessly curious man in history.'"

Allow me one last piece of advice—*you need to stay curious*—curious about your kids, curious about knowledge, curious about the curriculum, curious about best ways to teach and prepare curriculum and lessons.

See each student, each class, each year as unique, because they are. Be an anthropologist in your own classroom. Constantly observe your students; ask them questions about what is important to them how they spend their time, why they like what they like, and why they do what they do. If you do this throughout your career, you will find your students to be endlessly fascinating and teaching perpetually rewarding.

Teaching is a journey, one that never ends. You will never know it all; you will never master it all. Those are not the goals. *The goal is to keep learning;*

_ *ɴeep getting better.* Once again a reminder: *the goal is progress—not perfection!*

In doing that, both you and your students will be well served throughout your entire career as an educator.

Enjoy the trip!

TWENTY-NINE ESSENTIAL TRUTHS ABOUT TEACHING

1. Kids don't learn well from teachers they don't like.
2. We like kids who are like us—and we really like kids who are a lot like us. This can be a problem.
3. The only "black and white" you will find in teaching will be on the pages of a textbook. The rest are shades of gray.
4. Once your students like and respect you, they will not want to disappoint you. Then you can really teach them!
5. You can't free a fish from water.
6. You never lose when you learn.
7. Don't confuse activity with achievement.
8. Your best teachers are your students.
9. Bait the hook to suit the fish.
10. Kids don't learn well on an empty stomach.
11. It is not your job to save them all.
12. There is no such thing as perfection in teaching—not in you, not in your teaching, and not in your students—so don't try to achieve perfection. You want *progress, not perfection.*
13. Every minute of every class is precious.
14. Ten minutes is a huge chunk of time.
15. You never get a second chance to make a first impression.
16. First, be a good animal.
17. Be patient with your students—they're not done yet.
18. Be patient with yourself as a teacher—you're not done yet.
19. Expect a little rebellion now and then—you may even want to support it.
20. "There are only three ways to teach a child. The first is by example, the second is by example, the third is by example." Albert Schweitzer.
21. Students are naturally curious—use this to your advantage in your teaching.
22. You can't go it alone.
23. Failing to prepare is preparing to fail.
24. The creator gave beginning teachers two eyes, two ears, but only one mouth. Perhaps he was trying to tell them to watch and listen twice as much as they talk.

25. Kids remember great stories and the lessons they teach far better than almost anything else.
26. If a kid asks you, "Why do we have to learn this?" and your response is, "Because it's in the curriculum," it's time to move on to something that is relevant to them.
27. There is nothing stronger than gentleness.
28. Grit, determination, perseverance, work ethic, and a good heart are much more important than talent when it comes to being a successful teacher.
29. Be like da Vinci and *stay curious.*

LASTLY: THE SECRET TO SUCCESS IN TEACHING

Actor Bryan Cranston is one of the most preeminent actors of our time. He won the Primetime Emmy Award for Outstanding Lead Actor four times; he has won the Golden Globe Award for Outstanding Lead Actor; he has won the Screen Actors Guild Award four times, a Tony Award for Best Actor in a Play . . . and the list goes on.

In his book, *A Life in Parts*, Cranston was asked about how he became so successful. His views on what it takes to be successful as an actor have much to teach us about what it takes to be a successful teacher. Cranston says:

> I don't mean to make it sound high-flown. It's not. It's discipline and repetition and failure and perseverance and dumb luck and blind faith and devotion. It's showing up when you don't feel like it, when you're exhausted and you think you can't go on. Transcendent moments come when you've laid the groundwork and you're open to the moment. They happen when you do the work. In the end, it's about the work.

(p. 3)

And there it is. The secret to success in teaching is this: There are no secrets, and there are no shortcuts to success in teaching. Don't waste your time looking for them. Success in teaching is the result of hard work, learning from your mistakes, commitment to your students, and an unrelenting focus on continually becoming better at your craft, showing up when you don't feel like it, and being there for your students—even when they don't deserve it.

That's all there is to it!

For all of the non-teachers who will tell you that teaching is easy—with its short days and lots of holidays—invite them to get a teaching degree and give it a try. To be a great teacher is—and will be throughout your entire career—a great deal of work. Good teaching is always going to be hard work, and anyone who tells you otherwise is either deceitful or delusional.

Having said that, however, if you have the calling to be a teacher, and if you are prepared to work hard at your craft all the years of your teaching, you will meet some really delightful kids, you will work with some wonderful colleagues, and you will most certainly have some great adventures.

And, amid all the hard work, you will find yourself laughing with students, laughing at students, and laughing at yourself. Please remember this: if you are teaching and you are not laughing—a lot, every day in your classroom— you are doing something wrong. Good teaching is a lot of fun!

So if you hear that call, if you choose to work hard, if you remember to laugh and have fun at this thing called teaching, you will have lived a life filled with meaning, joy, and purpose—a life well spent.

I wish you that kind of success in your teaching career.

Three Recommendations for Further Reading

The Successful Teacher's Survival Kit, with its eighty-three ideas to help you to be a better teacher, is by its very nature a sketch—a synopsis—of the many challenges you will face as a teacher and the various ways you can choose to approach these challenges. Choosing this short format was deliberate on my part. I wanted to create a book that was quick, easy, and fun to read—and yet at the same time a book that offered proven suggestions that work in classrooms and with kids, suggestions that can help you become a successful teacher.

When you are ready to delve more deeply into some of these areas and you want more detail into ways to help you become better as a teacher, I highly recommend that you explore the following three books, all of which are listed in the reference section of this book.

Michael Linsin's *The Happy Teacher Habits: 11 Habits of the Happiest, Most Effective Teachers on Earth* (2016) is a fun yet educational read. Linsin takes you through some of the essential habits that help to make teachers successful. While there are certainly more than eleven habits that successful teachers practice, these eleven are a good basis. Take a look at Linsin's book and see how many of these habits you practice.

In another book by Linsin, *Dream Class: How to Transform Any Group of Students into the Class You've Always Wanted* (2014), goes into great detail in describing how he worked with challenging classes and challenging kids. His stories are interesting and right on target. Linsin clearly has a great deal of respect for students, and he demonstrates in detail how to establish non-negotiable boundaries for student behavior in your classroom—and what to do when a student chooses to step outside of these boundaries. You will find some of the same topics covered in Linsin's book as have been discussed here. However, he goes into greater detail than I have chosen to do here.

My last recommendation is Harry and Rosemary Wong's *The First Days of School: How to Be an Effective Teacher* (2009). Coming in at 346 pages, the Wongs again cover some of the same topics that are dealt with in this book, but they go into far greater detail. This book is well worth reading, especially if you are fairly new to teaching and want more specifics in regard to how to improve certain areas of your practice.

References

Ariely, Dan. (2016). *Payoff: The Hidden Logic That Shapes Our Motivations*. New York: Simon & Schuster.

Canfield, Jack, & Hansen, Mark Victor. (1993). *Chicken Soup for the Soul: 101 Stories to Open the Heart and Rekindle the Spirit*. Deerfield Beach, FL: Health Communications, Inc.

Cialdini, Robert. (2016). *Pre-suasion: A Revolutionary Way to Influence and Persuade*. New York: Simon & Schuster.

Coleman, P., & LaRocque, L. (1990). *Struggling to Be Good Enough*. Bristol, PA: The Falmer Press.

Covey, Stephen. (1989). *The Seven Habits of Highly Effective People*. New York: Simon & Schuster.

Cranston, Bryan. (2016). *A Life in Parts*. New York: Scribner.

Duane, Daniel. (2018, June 29). *How the Startup Mentality Failed Kids in San Francisco*. Retrieved from https://www.wired.com/story/willie-brown-middle-school-startup-mentality-failed/

Eiseley, Loren. (1978). *The Star Thrower*. New York: Random House.

Feinberg, Walter, & Soltis, Jonas. (1992). The Hidden Curriculum Revisited. In Feinberg, Walter, & Soltis, Jonas (Eds.), *School and Society* (2nd ed.), pp. 59–71. New York: Teachers College Press.

Ferreri, Laura, Bigand, Emmanuel, & Bugaiska, Aurélia. (2015). The Positive Effect of Music on Source Memory. *Musicae Scientiae*. Article first published online: September 8, 2015; Issue published: December 1, 2015. DOI: https://doi.org/10.1177/1029864915604684

Ginott, Haim. (1972). *Teacher and Child*. New York: The Macmillan Company.

Gladwell, Malcolm. (2005). *Blink: The Power of Thinking without Thinking*. New York: Little, Brown & Company.

Gladwell, Malcolm. (2009). *What the Dog Saw: And Other Adventures*. New York: Little, Brown & Company.

Greene, Maxine. (1973). *Teacher as Stranger*. Belmont, CA: Wadsworth Publishing Company.

Hanushek, Eric. (2014, April). *We Need Better Teachers*. Stanford Center for Education Policy Analysis. Retrieved from https://cepa.stanford.edu/news/we-need-better-teachers

Hanushek, Eric. (2014). Boosting Teacher Effectiveness. In Finn, Chester, Jr., & Sousa, Richard (Eds.), *What Lies Ahead for America's Children and Their Schools*. Stanford: Hoover Institution Press. Retrieved from http://www.hoover.org/sites/default/files/research/docs/finnsousa_whatliesahead_final_ch2.pdf

Harari, Yuval. (2016). *Sapiens: A Brief History of Humankind*. Canada: Random House of Canada Limited.

Isaacson, Walter. (2017) *Leonardo da Vinci*. New York: Simon & Schuster.

Kahneman, Daniel. (2011). *Thinking Fast and Slow*. Doubleday Canada.

Kalanithi, Paul. (2016). *When Breath Becomes Air*. New York: Random House.

Karweit, Nancy. (1984, May). Time on Task Reconsidered. *Educational Leadership*. The Association for Supervision and Curriculum Development, 32–35.

Lewis, Michael. (2017). *The Undoing Project: A Friendship That Changed Our Minds*. New York: W. W. Norton & Company, Inc.

Linsin, Michael. (2014). *Dream Class: How to Transform Any Group of Students into the Class You've Always Wanted*. San Diego, CA: JME Publishing.

Linsin, Michael. (2016). *The Happy Teacher Habits: 11 Habits of the Happiest, Most Effective Teachers on Earth*. San Diego, CA: JME Publishing.

Lortie, Dan. (1975). *Schoolteacher: A Sociological Study*. Chicago: University of Chicago Press.

McRaven, William H. (2017). *Make Your Bed: Little Things That Can Change Your Life . . . and Maybe the World*. New York: Grand Central Publishing.

Mitchell, Stephen (1988). *Tao Te Ching: A New English Version* (A translation of the Tao Te Ching by Lao-tzu). New York: HarperCollins Publishers.

Nicols, Tom. (2017). *The Death of Expertise: The Campaign against Established Knowledge and Why It Matters*. New York: Oxford University Press.

Noddings, Nel. (1989, March). *Developing Models of Caring in the Professions*. Paper presented at the Annual Meeting of the American Educational Research Association, San Francisco, California.

Orlick, Terry. (2008). *In Pursuit of Excellence*. Champaign, IL: Human Kinetics.

Palmer, Parker. (2000). *Let Your Life Speak: Listening for the Voice of Vocation*. San Francisco: Jossey-Bass.

Parables of Ramakrishna: The Parable of the Snake That Refused to Hiss. Retrieved September 23, 2018, from https://en.wikisource.org/wiki/Parables_of_Ramakrishna/The_Parable_of_the_snake_that_refused_to_hiss

Peale, Norman Vincent. (1956). *The Power of Positive Thinking*. Retrieved from http://www.makemoneywithpyxism.info/joinstevehawk.com/PowerOfPositiveThinking.pdf

Pierson, Rita. (2013, May). *Ted Talks: Every Kid Needs a Champion* [Video file]. Retrieved from https://www.ted.com/talks/rita_pierson_every_kid_needs_a_champion

Ripley, Dale. (2016). *What Makes a Teacher Great?* Unpublished paper, University of Alberta.

Rowe, Mary Budd. (1972, April). Wait-Time and Rewards as Instructional Variables: Their Influence on Language, Logic, and Fate Control. In Resources in Education, Education Resources Information Center. Presented at the National Association for Research in Science Teaching, Chicago, Illinois. Retrieved from http://eric.ed.gov/?id=ED061103

Sheehan, George. (1978). *Running and Being: The Total Experience*. New York: Simon & Schuster.

Stahl, Robert. (1994). Using "Think-Time" and "Wait-Time" Skillfully in the Classroom. *ERIC Digest*. Retrieved from http://files.eric.ed.gov/fulltext/ED370885.pdf

Tzu, Sun. (2011). *The Art of War*. Translation by James Trapp. New York: Chartwell Books, Inc.

Wehby, J., & Lane, K. (2009). *Behavioral Interventions in Schools: Evidence-Based Positive Strategies*. Washington, DC: American Psychological Association.

Wong, H., & Wong, R. (2009). *The First Days of School: How to Be an Effective Teacher*. Singapore: Harry K. Wong Publications, Inc.

Wooden, John. (1997). *Wooden: A Lifetime of Observations and Reflections on and off the Court*. Lincolnwood, IL: Contemporary Books.

About the Author

Dale Ripley, PhD, has more than thirty-five years of teaching experience working with students in elementary, junior high-middle, and high schools in the inner city, the suburbs, and on a First Nations reserve. While Dr. Ripley has been the principal of several schools and served two school districts as their superintendent, the classroom was—and still is—his favorite place to be. He is currently teaching in the Departments of Elementary and Secondary Education at the University of Alberta.